Tethering to Significance

Tethering to Significance

PREPARING TODAY'S LEADERS FOR TOMORROW'S CHALLENGES IN AN INCREASINGLY UNTETHERED CULTURE

Michael A. Hovda

Published by Amazon Kindle Direct Publishers

For the benefit of the reader, the Author has chosen to use many attributions accessible online as opposed to hardcopy, for ease of access. Because of the dynamic nature of the internet, any web addresses or links contained in this book may have changed since publication and may no longer be valid.

ISBN-13: 9781733040303
9781733040310

Printed in the United States of America

Dedicated to my bride of forty-seven years and counting,
Marilyn,
whom I do not deserve.

The times, they are a-changin'.
—Bob Dylan

Contents

Preface ···xiii

Introduction ·· xv

How to Read a Book ···xix
...*or at least this one.*

Chapter 1   The Credibility Question·······································1
Who cares? Why should I listen to Hovda?

Chapter 2   Secrets to Easy Leadership ·································7
How can I easily become an effective leader?

Chapter 3   Courage to Be Different·····································9
Calling a thermometer a "thermostat" doesn't make it a thermostat.

Chapter 4   Promotion—Now What? ····································23
Help! I am now "one of them."

Chapter 5   Life Lesson from a Flight Instructor····················31
Precisely navigating with an unreliable compass.

Chapter 6   Embracing Change, and Tradition ·····················41
Seven words of a dying career.

Chapter 7   A Seminal Career Tip: Leading Change · 49
Leveraging the power of the first follower.

Chapter 8   Critical Thinking, or Lack Thereof · 59
Thoughts on thinking.

Chapter 9   A Meds-Free Stress Control · 67
Assuming noble intent.

Chapter 10   Subconsciously Motivating Others · 77
Embracing intrinsic value.

Chapter 11   Stress-Free Delegation, or at Least Minimized · · · · · · · · · · · · · · · · · · 83
Strategy for tackling the number-one reason supervisors fail.

Chapter 12   Communicating Is Not Dueling Soliloquies · 91
Secrets to ratcheting up your verbal credibility.

Chapter 13   Meetings. Really? · 103
Quit taking minutes and stealing hours.

Chapter 14   Making Peace with Conflict · 111
How to win the person and not just the point.

Chapter 15   Untidy Organizational Skills · 123
The ability to retrieve.

Chapter 16   Customers Are Number One. It's a Lie! · 129
You can't display what you don't possess.

Chapter 17   Team Building or Cat Herding · 133
Why are we still trying to row the boat faster with the anchor out?

Chapter 18   Political Savvy: It Is Not What You Think · 143
*Learn how to engage politically without feeling the need to
shower afterward.*

Chapter 19   Time Management, and Other Myths · · · · · · · · · · · · · · · 151
              It is time to get serious!

Chapter 20   What Is...What Is to Be · 157
              Process and purpose!

              Appendix A Peer-Leadership Quotations · · · · · · · · · · · · 161

              Appendix B My GPS Action Plan · · · · · · · · · · · · · · · · 167

              Appendix C Testimonials · 169

              Acknowledgments · 175

              Notes · 177

Preface

Have you authored a book yet?

It has been a doggedly annoying question—a question that has nagged me through the decades. It has been asked by training participants, clients, colleagues, and friends, but curiously, not by family members. They apparently know me all too well. Don't misunderstand me; it's not like there has been a cry from the masses. You know how it goes—if you're told that you have potential when you're thirty years old, it's encouraging. However, if you're told that you have potential when you're sixty, that is discouraging. In my case, it's the latter.

To be clear, it isn't the question that is annoying; it's the answer. Each time I faced the question, I felt a twinge of failure behind the flattery. The discouraging part was that I kept succumbing to the wily seductions of lethargy and procrastination. The encouraging part was that apparently someone thought I might have something of value to say. That is still in question. I have had the privilege of serving as an executive coach to a wide spectrum of people, including university presidents, CEOs, and a governor. It was quite perplexing to me that they wanted my perspective, let alone paid me for it. Did I mention that my wife shares my perplexity?

So, here is how we are going to do it. You've heard the old phrase "one beggar telling another beggar where the bread is." That is how this book is going down. Picture yourself sitting across from me at Starbucks sipping on a caramel macchiato. Venti, that is. (If you need a picture in your mind, look at my photo on the back cover. I look just like Brad Pitt. OK, maybe not *just* like him!) You have been in the workplace for years now and are a seasoned leader. Or maybe you've just finished hanging that freshly inked diploma on your wall and you are now ready to jump into the workplace. Regardless, we are just going to have a conversation about things that matter.

Things like life, career, promotions, friends, meaning, work, people, hopes, difficulties, change, stress, conflict, meetings, failure, generations, communication, fears, etc. All these things are centered around influence, or as it is more commonly known, leadership. Hopefully you will discover practical tools and techniques as well as a few Yoda-like morsels that will lodge in your memory. However, if at the end of this book you conclude that it is more accurate to suggest that I have the wisdom of Brad Pitt but the appearance of Yoda, then I still wish you all the best!

My solitary ambition is this: that you—and those you influence—are better by the time you finish reading the last chapter. It is my hope that you will become smarter, more courageous, more determined, more focused, more empathetic, more effective, more ambitious, more content, and more tethered to significance.

Lastly, thank you for letting me seep into your life through this book. Whenever someone lets their guard down just enough to let me in, I consider that hallowed ground.

Introduction

Tethering to Significance
A GPS for tomorrow's leader.

Not another book on leadership! *Why should I invest my dime and time in another book on leadership?*

Maybe you shouldn't.

This book is only for those who can identify with one or more of the following leadership challenges. If you can't, then save your dime and time and invest in a good movie.

However, if you can see yourself in one or more of these challenges, then you may find significant returns on the pages to follow. And these returns aren't even taxable. Check out your potential ROIs (return on investment):

Greater promotional opportunities: Discover what skills, traits, behaviors, and attitudes tomorrow's decision-makers are looking for in their leaders, and how you can acquire them. Whether you are a rookie or veteran leader, or whether you work in the public or private sector, this book is for you. Hang on, because "the times they are a-changin'" and you need to be ready for what's coming.

Increased effectiveness: Learn how you can make a significant and lasting difference with your efforts, whatever those efforts may be.

Increased efficiency: Realize how you can do more with less, and do it faster.

Decreased stress: Discover the practical secrets to minimize your stress level in the midst of an increasingly stressful culture. Learn how to develop a long-term strategy to avoid professional and personal burnout.

Verbal credibility: Develop the ten techniques that will incite people to listen and respond to what you have to say.

Personal significance: Most important, discover how to capture a fresh and real connection to meaning in what you do.

To invest or not invest, that is the question. Still unsure? It may help to ask yourself if any of the following leader descriptions fit you:

Time-debt leader: All they are asking of me is to do more, with fewer resources, and to get it done faster. Every day I come to work feeling I owe people time from yesterday. How do I practically get out of time debt?

Politically reluctant leader: I thought if I just took responsibility for my outcomes that I would be noticed and appreciated, and that my career would develop accordingly. Little did I know, that is not how it works. It's more Machiavelli than meritocracy here. I see others who are less effective and less efficient getting the kudos, not to mention the promotions. It seems like I must resign myself to a minimized influence and a stagnated career, or I must abandon my principles and jump into the political swamp. How do I effectively and yet ethically increase my political influence without feeling like I have to take a shower after work?

Change-exhausted leader: I can't get my breath. It seems like the latest flavor of the month can't even wait until the next month to be announced. How do I navigate through the rapid currents of change and keep my head above water?

Conflict-aversion leader: It is so difficult to correct underperformers. Already I am starting to see my underperformers taking advantage of my reluctance, and worse yet, my high performers are starting to slack off. I mean, why can't we all just do our work, and everyone get along? Is there a way to confidently address difficult issues and still be liked?

Motivation-free leader: It's not me, it's them. I am motivated but I just can't seem to get people engaged. I would be a great leader if I just had different people on my team. I mean, they are getting paid to work, so why should I have to motivate them to be engaged?

Generationally restricted leader: I have been doing this for years, but it is more difficult today than ever. It seems like they just don't make people like they used to. I have millennials that think the state of change has always been humanity's tradition. They can't even remember dialing a phone with their fingers. I mean, they came out of the womb flexing their thumbs. At the same time, I have boomers that are sliding for home. How do I successfully supervise across the generational lines?

Emerging leader: I didn't see that coming. When I was promoted, I assumed that because I managed my work well, I would be able to manage the workers well. Now I find myself overwhelmed, possibly because I micromanage. I am constantly answering questions because I am incorrectly delegating, and I am frustrated by my own inefficiency due to my possessive problem solving. There must be more to leadership than firefighting. How do I successfully transfer my impact from work-management skills to people-management skills?

Pressured leader: This change initiative would fit neatly in my *Really Stupid Ideas* folder and now they are asking me to lead it. How do I get people to buy into a change that I haven't even bought into myself?

Organization-free leader: I just can't get my act together. I find myself spending way too much time trying to find it and I often feel completely disheveled. I'm not really a candidate for the *Hoarders* show yet, but my lack of organization is now adversely impacting my team. I don't even want to talk about prioritizing multiple projects. Am I fixable, or did this deficiency come on my personal hard drive?

Rodney Dangerfield leader: "I don't get no respect." When I talk, nobody listens. They step on my lines, they change the subject, or they simply don't respond. Occasionally, I hear the proverbial "interesting idea," but that's as far as it goes. How can I learn to speak so people want to hear what I have to say?

Paralyzed-presenter leader: I admit it. I hate talking in front of people. I feel that I have so much to offer, but my impact, and probably my career, are being throttled because I have so much difficulty with public presentations. How can I minimize my stress level, increase my fluency, and learn to speak on my feet?

Time-thief leader: I can hear my team at the watercooler after my meetings. "Now, what are we supposed to be doing? When is it supposed to be done by? Who is supposed to be doing it?" How do I keep my meetings from being a place where we keep minutes but steal hours?

Leaderless leader: I am supposed to be training future leaders, but I simply don't know where to turn. I've perused leadership/supervisor materials and it is daunting. It's like trying to locate a single snowflake in a winter storm. I just end up feeling like a deer in the headlights. Where can I get a solid, accurate, and practical resource for my aspiring leaders/supervisors? (OK, maybe this one is a crass advertisement for this book, but you will find it to be a great resource, and I will even show you how to do it!)

So, if you can't identify with any of these, then enjoy your movie. If you can identify, then hang on. You may be in for a good read.

How to Read a Book

Here are some ideas on how to squeeze the most value out of this book. First, consider it a *desktop reference tool*. Use it as...

- your personal how-to guide
- a curriculum for teaching your team
- mentoring material

Don't confuse *inspiration* with *inspired*. Hopefully these paper pages will generate some inspiration, but these pages are made of paper, not tablets of stone. So, here is the deal—make the book your personal learning tool. Its value to you is in the concepts, techniques, and tools, rather than the hallowed white pages. It is not bound in leather and you are not likely to include it in your will, so *make it work for you.*

Here is what I am talking about.

Become your own editor. Cross out that which is irrelevant and add that which is. However, keep in mind that while a concept may seem irrelevant or trivial now, in time it may prove to be the opposite.

Underline or highlight. We tend to increase our memory when we underline, circle, or highlight, so jump right in and mark it up.

Make notes in margins. Add your ideas, observations, and applications. Join me in authoring your book.

Dog-ear pages. You may want to quickly locate some pages in the future. Mark those pages with a dog-ear. Go ahead and bend that corner over. This may be painful for you, but you can do it. I checked with your mom and she said it was all right this one time, so dog-ear away.

Complete the exercises. I don't like to do them either, but I am often glad I did. Jump right in and tackle that exercise. The value you gain might surprise you.

Skip it. You heard me. Don't waste your time with excessive or redundant information. If you have that concept down or if it isn't relevant to your experience, then skip it. You don't need *more* information; you need *relevant* information.

Tear out pages. That's right—rip them out. If a page contains a concept that your boss would love, then tear it out and give it to her. If it contains an illustration that you want to use at your next meeting, then tear it out and bring it with you. If it contains a behavior that you want to teach your team, then tear it out and teach away. If it contains a high-level truth that you want to integrate personally, then tear it out and tape it to your desk. If you have greasy fingers after eating at Chick-fil-A and you don't have a napkin, then tear it out and...well, maybe not. There is a greater likelihood that you will use the content if you tear out the page than if you wait until you finish the book and then try to remember where it was and how you were going to use it. Besides, I know where you can get more books if you need them.

Bookmark it. Along with this book comes its own bookmark. You will find in appendix B a page titled "GPS Action Sheet." Tear it out. No, I mean right now—tear it out now. This will be your bookmark. Consider this: A map just gives a silent panoramic view of a territory. A GPS, on the other hand, will audibly and visually guide you from point A to point B. It actually tells you how to get there step by step. Tear it out and create your personal leadership GPS!

CHAPTER 1

The Credibility Question

Who cares? Why should I listen to Hovda?

Writing a book is a horrible, exhausting struggle,
like a long bout of some painful illness.
One would never undertake such a thing
if one were not driven on by some demon
whom one can neither resist nor understand.
—George Orwell

So what? you may be asking. *Why should I listen to you?* Good question. I would ask the same.

Introduction

Let me introduce myself. My name is Mike, and I would like to have a conversation with you about what leadership will look like in the future, how that future will affect you, and how you can get ahead of the curve by preparing yourself. If you were my kid entering the work environment, then this is the conversation that we would have.

If the "so-what" factor is unimportant to you, then skip to chapter 2 and I will meet you there shortly. Just a caution, doing so may cause some head-scratching in future chapters!

Credibility

If you have jumped ahead and peeked at my bio on the back cover, then you already know by my hairstyle that I am an old geezer. I am playing the back nine of life. Yup, I have been teaching leadership-related subjects in some form for the last four decades throughout forty-nine states and six countries. I have been privileged to access multiple communication venues such as teaching, counseling, lecturing, preaching, debating, consulting, and writing. In fact, I have been privileged to work with leaders across both the public and private sectors, as well as the civilian and military sectors. This includes both emerging and seasoned leaders, from the Pentagon to the White House, and from the Federal Executive Institute to the World Trade Center. You get the picture—I have been around the proverbial block.

Journey

Years ago, I worked for a national training organization. They would send me to hotels and conference centers, and I would train employees from a variety of organizations. Some of those employees would return to their organizations and personally recommend me, which led to invitations for me to design and facilitate in-house training courses for them. These opportunities gave me a rich and eclectic experience in personnel development which I value to this day.

However, it was also very perplexing and quite frustrating. It became apparent over time that these trainings had little lasting impact. The surveys were strong, and the participants were generous with their praise, but the training didn't seem to make much of a lasting impact. This spawned in me a frustration-tinged curiosity. How was it that the material and the facilitation were so well received but the impact was so short lived?

Initially there was a brief temptation on my part just to soak in the accolades and cash my checks, but it was fleeting. I found little interest in becoming a paid information dump truck. I had to make a difference.

So, I invested serious thought into why so much of traditional training had such little impact over the long term. More importantly, I asked myself what I could do differently that would create a longer-lasting impact. It then began to dawn on me: Almost all of the leadership-related courses that I had been teaching contained content that was really relevant to my participants' everyday lives, but they were being taught and applied within the confines of the eight-to-five workday window. I was teaching leadership-related courses on conflict-management skills, communication skills, supervision skills, motivation skills, organizational skills, project-management skills, time-management skills, delegation skills, negotiation skills, etc. It became apparent to me that most of these skills were also necessary in their 24/7 life; not just their eight-to-five work life.

So, I took a leap. I quit. I dumped much of what I had learned about training and began to develop a fresh approach to personal development. I served out my year of non-compete and launched my own company called Hovda and Associates, Inc. - InsideOutLeadership. It was a huge leap, but like many budding entrepreneurs, I was full of passion and optimism.

I knew that the most important relationships that people have are their family and friends. So, I began to design and facilitate the courses by constructing traction points within their 24/7 life and then transferring that skill to their eight-to-five work window. For instance, if that participant saw the value and relevance of conflict management within the family unit, then it made sense that they would be more willing to integrate that skill into their work environment, and that it would become a learned instinct over time. It was a big gamble, but I leaped out with unearned confidence.

I crashed and burned. If it hadn't been for my patient, albeit hungry wife, I would have quit. I patiently persisted, and in time it paid off. I was contacted by a Fortune 100 organization that was creating a new company. This new company was the result of two merging companies with totally different cultures. They asked me to design and facilitate a two-day leadership workshop for their senior managers. I held my nose, grabbed my shiny new training approach, and jumped in with both feet. It could not have gone better. I soon became the primary trainer for the organization and worked almost full time for close to five years, until the company was sold. The organization's employees scattered to other organizations and brought my name with them. The rest is history.

Philosophy

I heard that yawn. *So what, exactly, is this inside-out training philosophy*, you might ask? By *philosophy* I mean this unique (some would say eccentric) approach to instructional design, training, coaching, and consulting.

Think about how we hire and fire in our culture. We essentially hire people because we confirm the presence of three desirable components: education, experience, and practical skills. I refer to these three as the **H3**.

We review the applicant's resume or CV looking for the presence of the **H3**. We interview the applicant, listening for the presence of the **H3**. We scrutinize referrals, searching for the presence of the **H3**. Regardless of the position, regardless of the level, regardless of the trade, regardless of the sector, these three criteria seem to have risen to the top of our hiring filter.

But stop and think about it. Don't we struggle with employees for entirely different reasons? Certainly, the **H3** are essential to performance outcomes, but isn't performance seeping out through ignored cracks?

Consider this: You know that person who has been with the company for years? Let's call him Rick. I am talking about the one who has incredible organizational knowledge. The one who is the go-to person when information is needed. The one who deeply possesses the **H3**. And yet, he is absolutely toxic! Few can stand Rick. His colleagues despise him, his boss begrudgingly tolerates him, and even the customers endure him. He seems to get away with mistreating just about everyone who crosses his path and yet no one seems to hold him accountable. He is the personification of misery. His primary virtue is generosity, for he shares his misery wherever he goes.

So, why do we continue to tolerate the intolerable Ricks? Why? Because there is a perception that they are too valuable of a resource to offend, let alone fire. Let me encourage you by saying that those days are coming to an end.

Some performance-pioneering organizations have already come to the realization that the collateral damage that the Ricks create to their surrounding environment is now deemed greater than the value that their personal **H3** brings to the table. There is a net performance loss.

You know what I'm talking about. They ruin brainstorming sessions with their condescension. They crash the team's morale with their boorish behavior. They prompt colleagues to seek employment elsewhere with their annoying arrogance. They can demoralize their boss into an accountability surrender. In fact, the Ricks end up being the best salesmen…for the competitors. And yet, they possess strong education, experience, and practical skills.

Here is an easy test to identify a Rick. Does your meeting have a different atmosphere when he is absent? Does your work culture take a leap forward when he is on vacation? If so, that is probably your Rick.

However, Bob Dylan was right: "The times, they are a-changin.'" Sprinkled throughout your book will be examples, illustrations, and arguments as to what these "times are a-changin'" into, but let me give you one quick illustration. According to Government Executive, 30% of federal workers will be retirement age by 2023. In fact, four federal agencies, HUD, EPA, NASA, and Treasury, will have over 40% retirement age by that time.[1] Who will be replacing these exiting baby boomers? Millennials and

Gen Zers! This tectonic cultural shift is already taking place. Millennials are already having a much greater role in determining the culture of the work environment.

History stamps generations with unique traits. For instance, one of history's stamps on the baby boomers is debt. We left American culture with debt. (You're welcome!) One of history's emerging millennial stamps is their mooring to their work environment. By *mooring,* I mean the reason why they work for their employer. It can be summarized like this: *Millennials don't quit jobs—they quit people.* (More on the millennial stamps later!) We are discovering that many millennials have quit jobs that offer strong compensation and security, simply because of the toxic culture. They now happily work for organizations with healthy cultures, but with less compensation. If this stamp continues, and it is difficult to see why it would not, then we must refocus our work cultures. When *cultures* have a greater leverage on hiring and retaining than *compensation* has, then cultures will have to adapt. Healthy cultures will replace compensation-driven cultures as recruiting and retaining tools. (Can you hear Dylan in the background?)

So, you may ask, what does this have to do with the inside-out philosophy? I am glad you asked. Remember the **H3** criteria that we use for hiring—education, experience, and practical skills? I mentioned that we struggle with people for entirely different reasons. I propose that we struggle with people, and even fire them, because of the *absence* of three entirely different things. I call them the **F3**: effort, ethics, and people skills.

That's it. Performance is increasingly impacted by the influence of the **F3** rather than just the presence of the **H3**. The **H3** will always be essential—there will be no substitutes—but the evolving role of the **F3** will increasingly be forming our work cultures.

Going forward, let's rename the **F3** and call them the *pivotal intangibles* of high performers: effort, ethics and people skills. The inside-out approach addresses these pivotal intangibles, which reside deep within an individual.

Knowing this to be true, Hovda and Associates, Inc. has centered our personnel development philosophy on these pivotal intangibles. We still educate, we still provide experience opportunities, and we still provide practical skills in our training (and you will see these splashed across the pages), but it is all done with these pivotal intangibles wafting through the material, the exercises, the assessments, the illustrations, the projects, the presentation, and the follow-up.

That's right...I said follow-up. Although "one-and-done" is still the most common form of training, and we certainly do our share, follow-up is one of the best tools to salvage and leverage personnel development impact; not to mention your training dollar.

As a teaching leader, keep in mind that if you don't monitor it, you can't measure it, and if you can't measure it, then you can't manage it. Personnel development needs to be monitored, measured, and managed. Here is our four-step inside-out approach to personnel development through training.[2]

- **Receptivity**: How well did the participants respond to the training or coaching?
- **Retention**: How much did the participants remember after a designated time frame?
- **Routine**: What attitudes, perspectives, and behaviors became a part of the participants' learned instinct?
- **Results**: In what measurable way has the organization improved as a result of the participants' response to the training?

Summary—Here are the building blocks and best practices that will prepare you for tomorrow's leadership challenges.

- All good leaders are good teachers, so think through your development philosophy.
- There is a tectonic shift occurring in the workforce due to retiring Boomers being replaced by Millennials and Gen Zers.
- When recruiting, hiring, and promoting, consider the F3 (pivotal intangibles) rather than depending exclusively on the H3.
- View your employees as people, rather than just employees.
- Tether your personnel-development points to their 24/7 life, not just to their eight-to-five work window. Use the inside-out approach.
- Recognize the increasing power of *culture* over *compensation* when recruiting, hiring, training, and promoting.
- Develop a habit of monitoring and measuring personnel development, so you can manage accordingly.
- Follow up, follow up, and then follow up.

CHAPTER 2

Secrets to Easy Leadership

How can I easily become an effective leader?

I was young and foolish then;
now I am old and foolisher.
—MARK TWAIN

That's right—it ain't easy and there aren't any secrets! Here is your leadership challenge—roll up your sleeves, grab a fistful of ambition, and hang on.

CHAPTER 3

Courage to Be Different

Calling a thermometer a "thermostat" doesn't make it a thermostat.

The pessimist complains about the wind;
the optimist expects it to change;
the realist adjusts the sails.
—William Arthur Ward

Let's start with the end in mind. Tomorrow's leaders must know what tried and tested leadership components need to be retained, and what new leadership components must be acquired. Change is not synonymous with progress. It is my concern that we are laying aside some time-tested leadership truths to buy into the flavor-of-the month components, and at other times we cling to worn-out leadership practices while neglecting future-required components. The days of managers simply creating semiprogrammable robots are coming to an end.

For instance, one of these newer leadership components is the ability to lead reluctant people through change (more about this in chapter 7). Historically, this was not a significant tool in the leader's toolbox, but it will become a primary tool going forward. You already know it to be true, but we live in a rapidly changing world. Not only is change everywhere but the very *rate* of change is increasing. And staggering. The need for you to develop this skill will only escalate in time.

In this book we will walk through those time-tested components that you need to solidify, but we will also meld them with the new leadership components required to equip you for high-impact influence going forward.

Tethering to Significance

I know it's not popular to be entirely honest in a book but here it goes: I am a totally broken person and I have a closet. An ugly closet. It has some ugly junk in it consisting of things I regret, that I have said and done, and that I hope nobody finds out about. If they do, I hope they keep their mouth shut.

It gets even worse. You too are broken, and yes, you have a closet as well. So does everyone. You know that person who comes to work that you think has it all together? They don't! None of us do, and yet we go to work every day and act like we do. We all know how the game is played. Life is tough. It is difficult. But we pretend like we are not insecure and that we don't have any fears, when in fact we all do.

The leader of tomorrow realizes that every person essentially wants to know that they matter. They matter to somebody, somewhere. The high-impact leader of tomorrow not only understands this basic human need but learns how to connect this person to meaning. I call this connecting *tethering to significance*. In the pages to come, we will explore two aspects of this tether: 1) how you can cultivate this awareness and how to strengthen your own tethers to significance; and 2) how you can cultivate this awareness in others and strengthen their tethers to significance (think family, colleagues, bosses, and employees).

Let's start with a small but substantive illustration. Consider the tethering power of an authentic and timely compliment. I didn't say *flattery*, I said *compliment*. My voice is lonely in this context, but audibly spamming people with superficial niceties with the intent of making them feel good about themselves has short-term benefits but long-term costs. Think about it. What do you feel like when you know someone is flattering you? Don't you want to say something like "Just tell me what you want. Let's not walk through this little manipulative charade"? Flattery can gag a maggot.

However, an authentic and timely compliment can have the entirely opposite impact. It can become a small but very real tether to significance. Mark Twain said, "I can live for two months on a good compliment."[1]

I have been known in class to ask people how many have received a handwritten compliment from a boss. It could take the form of a thank-you note, it could be an email, or it could simply be written on a Post-it Note. Usually about 60 to 80% of the class raise their hands. Then I ask of those who have raised their hands, "How many of you still have that note?" It is usually about 70 to 80%! Finally I ask, "How long have you had it?" Then the stories begin to roll. One person pulled a crinkly, old paper from her purse—a compliment from a boss written years ago. Another person told me that he led a project a couple of decades earlier that turned out to be unexpectedly successful. As a result, his boss gave him a medal, a $5,000 bonus, and a handwritten compliment. He told me that he couldn't remember what he did with the money and that he didn't know where the medal was, but he had the handwritten compliment in his wallet.

The primary value of the authentic and timely compliment is not in how it makes us feel but something much deeper. We are made to achieve. In just about everything in our lives, we instinctively want better whether we realize it or not. Each time we strive to be or do better, we construct another tether to significance. It may be something small and seemingly mindless. If someone drops something, you pick it up and hand it to them. Why? You want to leave people and circumstances better than when you found them. When someone authentically compliments us for work well done, that compliment reminds us that we have achieved, and that connects us to significance, or meaning.

Just a thought about the false pursuit of happiness. Don't get me wrong—I am all for happiness. Winning the lottery would make us happy, getting a raise makes us happy, winning a game makes us happy, having circumstances line up in the path of our life makes us happy. But happiness is not where it's at—significance or meaning is. When the tough times come, and they always do, happiness will not carry us through. Tethering to meaning will. It is time we as leaders shift from motivating employees primarily with *happiness* tactics and start authentically building tethers to *significance*. (Are you listening, parents?)

Note: If you are starting to be concerned that Hovda is turning fluffy on you, let me assure you—that is not the case. I am certainly not on the fluff bandwagon. Superficial niceties have become a lazy counterfeit to authentic caring. Authentic caring deepens your relationships, superficial niceties cheapen them.

Leaders and Managers

Just so we are on the same page, before we start dissecting leadership, let's make certain we are looking at the same big picture of leadership.

Let's start here. Two terms that are often conflated are *management* and *leadership*. As you can imagine, both are commonly found in the same person, but that doesn't mean that they are interchangeable. This distinction is not insignificant.

Here is your first exercise. Think of the best boss you have ever known. Look in your life's rearview mirror and identify someone that you would describe as the best boss that you have known. I don't care if it's your existing boss or if it's a boss at

McDonald's when you were sixteen. I will make it easier for you. This boss doesn't even have to have been your boss, but they do need to be someone that you have observed. Write their name under the term **BEST BOSS** in Exhibit 3.1.

You know where we are going from here. Now write down the name of the worst boss that you have ever experienced under the term **WORST BOSS** in the table.

Just a couple of tips before you get started: It will probably be more valuable for you if the name of the Best Boss is someone other than yourself. Just saying. Also, think about who you will be loaning your book to before you record the name of your worst boss. A pseudonym may be appropriate.

<u>Step 1</u>: **BEST BOSS**: Tell me why you thought of this particular boss when I said, "Best Boss." What was it that drew your memory to him/her? One rule before you start writing. Write out your description of your best boss with one-word descriptors in the appropriate column. You can use as many descriptors as you want but each descriptor must be one word. Create as long a list as you want. Oh yeah, one more thing: It is timed. You have sixty seconds to record your **Best Boss** descriptors. Only your **Best Boss** for now. Ready? Go!

<u>Step 2</u>: **WORST BOSS**: You get the idea. Now work on your **Worst Boss**. Same instructions. You have sixty seconds to record your **Worst Boss** descriptors. Ready? Go!

<u>Analysis</u>

- Which boss was the easiest to describe? ___________________
- Which boss did you use the more graphic and stronger descriptors with? ___________________
- Now the big question: Look at your descriptors in both columns. How many of your descriptors refer directly or indirectly to *management skills* (delegation, project management, time management, organization, etc.) and how many refer directly or indirectly to *leadership traits* (honesty, trustworthy, listens, empathetic, etc.)? Which of the skill sets is most represented by the descriptors?

____

Did you find it easier to describe your worst boss? I thought so.

Are your Worst Boss descriptors a little more graphic? I thought so. My vocabulary has been increased by listening to participants complete the Worst Boss descriptors.

Did you use more leadership traits than management skills to describe your two leaders? I thought so. You must be typical. Even though I didn't say Best *Leader*, but

Exhibit 3. 1.	
BEST BOSS	**WORST BOSS**

rather, Best *Boss*, people still evaluate bosses based on leadership traits over management skills.

Warren Bennis was a time-tested leadership guru, a best-selling author, an advisor to US presidents, as well as a professor at Boston University, Harvard, and MIT. Here is how he addressed the management-leadership subject: "Failing organizations are usually over-managed and under-led."[2] In one respect, that is sad. However, in another respect, it's great. It's great for people like you who have an understanding and an interest in developing your contemporary traits and skills.

Let's take it down a level. Here are four contrasting points that you want to hang on to in order to clarify the distinctions between management and leadership. It's not that one is superior to the other. Both are needed, but they differ in essence, they differ in utilization, and they differ in outcomes.

Managers see employees but leaders see people.
Does that sound like a training PowerPoint cliché, or what? Probably. But there actually is a substantive point lurking under the superficial reading. Later, in chapter 11, we will explore this in depth, but right now consider this: Do we need managers that monitor, measure, and manage employee performance? Absolutely! But how often do you see it where a boss tries to improve the performance of an underperforming employee simply by using management techniques and tools? It often leads to a disappointing outcome. A manager with strong leadership skills provides employees with tethers that help modify their behavior.

Managers design plans but leaders create vision.
Hang on to this one! People tend to buy into vision but rarely buy into plans. There are impressive managers who can construct exhaustive plans that consider a variety of moving parts. They squeeze their impressive planning skills inside of a PERT Chart and command a massive project. That is good management.

Consider this: You decide to build a house. The architect rolls out the blueprints. You can see how big the kitchen is in relation to the great room. You can see where the fireplace is going to be located. You notice window placement, room locations, and room proportions. You start to get excited. But then…she puts up the colored drawing of the finished house on the flip chart. The full power of the curb appeal leaps out. I mean, it has the finished landscaping with a robin sitting in a mature oak tree and smoke coming out of the chimney. The curb appeal is stunning. You say, "That's what I'm talking about!" That is your vision!

There are some leaders that can paint impressive verbal pictures of vision that induce broad buy-in. That is good leadership.

People tether to vision rather than plans.

On August 28, 1963, Dr. Martin Luther King, Jr. significantly moved the civil rights needle with a seventeen-minute speech at the Lincoln Memorial in Washington, D.C. He could have said, "I have a plan. First, we are going to develop an educational strategy that will be implemented within elementary schools across the country. Second, we will submit legislation designed to put policies in place that will…" But he didn't. He simply said, "I have a dream."[3] He continued to word-paint, "…*little children will one day live in a nation where they will not be judged by the color of their skin, but by the content of their character. I have a dream.*" Who could not buy into that picture?

"I have a plan" just wouldn't cut it.

Managers excel in times of complexity, but leaders excel in times of chaos.[4] Complexity and chaos require different skills.

There are impressive managers who can take highly complicated challenges and construct complex solutions to solve these challenges. That is good management.

But leaders have developed the insights and the instincts to point where we should go when we march off the edge of the map. When the crises hit and there is no guiding protocol or policy, the leader takes initiative. That is good leadership.

Managers wield positional authority, but leaders wield personal authority.
Your positional authority resides in the trappings of your position, like title, job description, corner office, etc. Your personal authority resides in who you are as a person.

If as a boss you face insubordination by an employee, you must defend your positional authority whether you feel like it or not. If that positional authority is lost, then structure collapses. Positional authority can take a variety of postures (see chapter 17 for more information), but it still must exist in some form.

Try this out. In every classroom I've visited, regardless of the continent, I have asked the participants to complete the following sentence. Now you give it a try.

People are willing to follow someone that they ___________________.

Let me guess. You said "trust." Or you may have said "admire," or possibly "respect." One of the fascinating things about this simple exercise is what people do *not* say. Almost never does someone say "like."

Do you know someone that you really like, but you wouldn't follow them around the block? Do you know someone that is not very high on your birthday-card list, but you would follow them anywhere?

Your positional authority connects with an employee; your personal authority tethers to a person. Remember—you give your employees a performance evaluation once a year, but they give you a performance evaluation every day. It is displayed by how much they respect and respond to you as a leader.

What do you think? Is trust difficult to construct? You bet. Second question: Is it difficult to maintain? Again, you bet. In some respects, it may be even more difficult to maintain than to construct. Long-term relationships in any spectrum of life are challenging. Many of us have short-term relationships littering our wake, oftentimes the result of the violation of trust. Third question: Is trust difficult to destroy? Have you ever met anyone who would answer this with a "yes"? We know instinctively and experientially that trust is easy to destroy. Final question: Is trust difficult to reconstruct once it has been violated? Absolutely—it is probably more difficult than constructing or maintaining it. Once you build it, invest even greater effort and courage in maintaining it.

Trust leaves on horseback but returns on foot. (Anonymous)

Thermometers and Thermostats

In some respects, it is more difficult to be a leader today than it was when I was young, and it won't be getting easier. Our culture is moving away from a more authoritarian form of leadership toward a more democratic form. Parents used to rely on a simple phrase to get their kids to respond to their wishes: "Because I said so." It seemed to work in any situation. Not so much anymore. Elementary teachers used to possess an assumed authority. You did not want to cross your teacher, or a price would be paid. (I may or may not be speaking from experience.) Today, parents are becoming friends with kids, and elementary teachers are becoming facilitators with their students. Contemporary structures are less supportive of authoritarian leaders, and in some cases undercut them.

Let me be clear—I am not pining for the good old days. In some respects, this is a healthy transition, but in other respects, it can be harmful; regardless, it will be challenging. (More about that in chapter 17.) George Orwell warned us, "Every generation imagines itself to be more intelligent than the one that went before it, and wiser than the one that comes after it."[5] Each exiting generation concludes that they just don't make youth like they used to, so we all need to be careful about overreaching with generational conclusions. Regardless, the fact is that today's leaders must construct their own individual traction points of influence. You are not going to get much assistance from existing structures and institutions. This can be intimidating. Tomorrow's leader will have to salmon his or her way up the cultural stream and this will require confidence. Specifically, the confidence to be different.

On a personal note, I want to encourage you to determine to be confident as you face your future. When I say encourage, I am not referring to this frothy connotation of wanting a person to feel better about oneself in their existing state. I am leaning more on the denotation of infusing courage in another to enable them to move to a more desired state.

Confidence is the selection of small chunks of courage on a daily basis. Every day we are confronted with stepchildren of fear like criticism, doubt, unrealistic deadlines, resource scarcity, shifting demands, personnel shortages, relationship challenges, irate bosses, personal insecurities, duplicitous colleagues, insubordinate employees, etc. How you choose to respond to these stepchildren of fear will either construct layers of confidence or it will strip them away. Repeatedly choosing courage on a regular basis builds a strong foundation of confidence.

When our oldest daughter, Rachel, was about two years old, I placed her up high on our living room steps. I stood below her with outstretched arms and told her to "jump to Dad." (Apparently her mom wasn't home at the time.) Blessed with good judgment, she refused. So, I put her on the second lowest step and repeated the request. Without hesitation, she jumped. I moved her to the third step and again repeated the request with the same response. Each time she moved up a step until she was finally on the original high perch. This time, without hesitation, she jumped at my request. Confidence is the result of selecting small chunks of courage on a daily basis.

Let's look at this idea about courage from another angle. The US military is one of our culture's most trusted institutions. Americans place more trust in the military than any of the other fourteen societal institutions included in the Gallup polling. It has held this position for decades and with good reason. According to Gallup polling in June of 2018, 74% of Americans trusted the military. (See Exhibit 3. 2.)[6] Sadly, there are only three institutions remaining that have a net positive (i.e., over 50%) trust factor.

Exhibit 3. 2.

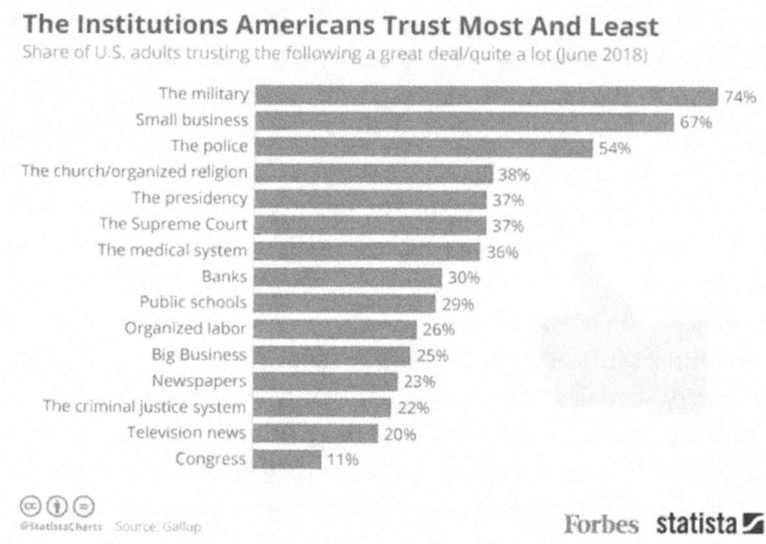

My Personal Bias: A Brief Aside

Full disclosure: I have a bias. I have been privileged to work for all five branches of our Armed Forces and have taught leadership courses at the Pentagon. I have been privileged to work with some of our outstanding existing and future leaders.

I'd like to take just a moment to make a selfish shout-out to those active and retired warriors and to their families—all of whom have served: Thank you.

In 1962, we were at the height of the Cold War when a Central Intelligence Agency U-2 spy plane picked up photographic evidence of the construction of Soviet ballistic missile facilities being constructed in Cuba, less than ninety miles from US soil. President John F. Kennedy, on October 22, 1962, established a naval blockade around Cuba, which constituted an act of war. Some historians believe that it was the closest that the world has come to nuclear war since Nagasaki on August 9, 1945. For thirteen days, the world held its breath as Soviet leader Nikita Khrushchev and Kennedy worked behind the scenes to negotiate a peaceful settlement. Finally, Khrushchev backed down and the sites were dismantled.

The world let out a sigh of relief. On November 26, 1962, President JFK went down to Fort Stafford, GA, to speak to the First Armored Division and to thank them for their part in the blockade. In his short speech, he quoted a variation of a poem written by an old warrior-poet who once wrote, he quoted an old warrior-poet who once wrote...

> God and soldiers all men adore
> In times of trouble and then no more.
> When war is over and all wrongs righted.
> God is neglected and the old soldier slighted.

It is a sad country where citizens marinate in peace and freedom, oblivious to the price so many have paid and continue to pay. It is encouraging to see that this country's citizens appear to continue to "adore" those who pay the price. I stand proudly in that 74% represented in the Gallup poll.

Colin Powell is one of America's more revered leaders in our most trusted institution. He is a retired four-star general, former Commander of the US Army Forces Command, former Chairman of the Joint Chiefs of Staff, and former Secretary of State. He was asked by a White House Fellow to "define the key characteristics of effective leadership that allow you to be an advocate for good." His rapid-fire, one-word response was "trust."[7] He went on to explain that everything he learned about leadership came from his sergeant at the Infantry School at Fort Benning, GA, decades ago. The sergeant told him, "You know you are good leader when people follow you, if only out of curiosity." General Powell went on to say, "I have never had a better definition." The sergeant went on to explain, "No matter how cold it is, you must never look cold. No matter how hungry you all are, you must never appear hungry. No matter how terrified you are, you must never look terrified. Because if you are scared, terrified, hungry, and cold, they will be scared, terrified, hungry, and cold." You cannot influence unless you have the courage to be different.

One of the leadership skills most emphasized in recent times has been team building, and rightfully so. Both the sports term and its concepts have been adopted by the military, federal agencies, private sector companies, NGOs, and even educational institutions. It is important that we work together toward a common mission, and I have certainly contributed my part to advancing team building. However, the overemphasis on team building has contributed to groupthink and Lemming-leadership.

You cannot influence that which is of the same substance. Salt can only season that which is not salt. You must have the courage to be different in order to make a difference. Tomorrow's leaders must be able to build teams while choosing to have the courage to be different when necessary.

Check out Exhibit 3. 3. If a leader is just like their team in every way, then they are *not* leading. A leader must have the courage to be a rebel. A rebel has the courage to be "other than." They can swim against the current. Unfortunately, the direction they are swimming is usually not in the team's best interest. On the other hand, the leader is not only "other than" like a rebel, but is also "more than." When everyone else is hungry, the leader doesn't act hungry. When there is a shortage of resources and everyone is complaining, the leader doesn't complain.

Exhibit 3. 3.

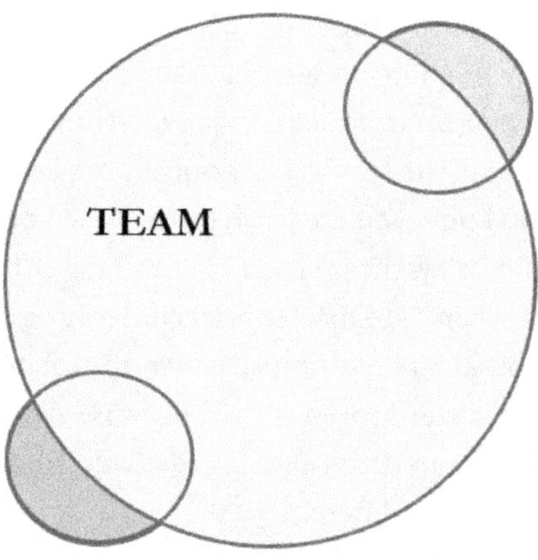

On your living room wall hangs an electric device that has two components. One is called a thermometer. Its sole purpose is to *reflect* the changes in the ambient environment. When the temperature goes up, it goes up. When the temperature goes down, it goes down. It follows the environment, or culture. The other component is called a thermostat. Its sole purpose is to *set* the temperature.

The leader of tomorrow must have the courage to be "more than"; to be a thermostat. To set the culture

Summary—Here are the building blocks and best practices that will prepare you for tomorrow's leadership challenges.

- Discipline yourself to start with the end in mind. Develop this into a habit by viewing small projects and responsibilities from this vantage point.
- Identify your tethers to significance by drafting a list of those things that generate purpose in your life. Be specific.
- Identify and strengthen your employees' tethers to significance.
- Review your Best Boss descriptors (see figure Exhibit 3. 1.) and convert them into your personal leadership goals.
- Strengthen your trust-builders and avoid your trust-busters.
- Establish the habit of clarifying and articulating your visions, not just your plans. Remember, most people are more inclined to buy into vision rather than plans.

- Strive to elevate your personal authority rather than relying solely on your positional authority. Solicit feedback from your boss, colleagues, employees, and family.
- Build your leadership confidence by choosing small chunks of courage on a daily basis. Remember, you can only learn bravery when fear is present.
- Choose to be a thermostat! Identify specific ways you can display that you are *Other Than* and *More Than* your team.

CHAPTER 4

Promotion—Now What?

Help! I am now "one of them."

> The greatest leader is not necessarily the
> one who does the greatest things.
> He is the one that gets the people to do the greatest things.
> —RONALD REAGAN

Suppose you have just been promoted and now you are the boss. Congratulations! You have now crossed the line and become one of *them*. Regardless of whether your title is team lead, director, or dictator, you will now be perceived by your former peers in a different light. You may encounter unexpected confusion and loneliness. Let's look at some of the transitions that today's leaders seem to find the most difficult, and let's develop some practical solutions.

Launching Your Culture

Note: The suggestions in this section are quite generic, but they should give you something to work with. There are many variables that could substantially modify these suggestions. Variables like inheriting a toxic team, starting a new team from scratch, supervising a team with nepotism, etc.

Launch your culture, not just your career. Yesterday you were *one of the guys* and now this morning you are one of *them*. In their minds you have changed. In your mind, you are the same. You may even feel a little apologetic for your newfound authority.

You may sense the pressure to convince them that you are the same, likeable person. You may want to launch a "good old boys (or girls)" culture.

Here is where I need to throw up a caution. Remember the *complete the sentence exercise* from chapter 3?

People are willing to follow someone that they <u>TRUST (not like)</u>.

Your team is not Facebook and your success will not be determined by how many likes or friends you get. Now, there are some "leaders" who have mastered the art of creating enemies. I am not talking about that. But your goal isn't to be liked—it is to be trusted. The two are not necessarily incompatible, but trust-building needs to trump like-building. Even Jesus said, "Woe to you when everyone speaks well of you" (Luke 6:26 NIV).

Here are six solutions that will help you launch your culture.

1. *Hold a candid conversation with your team.* Sit down with your new team as soon as possible and look them in the eye. Predetermine that you will be courageously humble but not cowardly weak. Explain to them what your vision is and what their role may be in achieving this vision. Make a point to listen and respond to each question or suggestion.
   - *Take notes.* This will help you remember and respond. It will also give the impression, accurately I hope, that you care about what they say. Be sure to follow up on the suggestions. If you don't use them, let them know why.
   - *Defend your new position but be personally vulnerable.* They will be watching you. If someone gets away with some unaddressed insubordination, then you may be unknowingly setting yourself up to be steamrolled. Memorize this statement: *Silence on my part in the face of unacceptable behavior will be perceived as approval.*
   - *Use strong meeting-management skills.* (See chapter 13 for these.) Your meetings are a microcosm of your management at large. Your new team will subconsciously draw conclusions about your expectations at large by the way you conduct your meeting.
2. *Hold a candid conversation with your competitor.* It is possible that someone you will now be supervising may very well have wanted your position. This can result in an awkward, if not tumultuous, relationship. Sit down with this person one-on-one in private and lay your cards on the table. Your actions may include the following.

- Audibly recognize that there could be an awkwardness in this relationship and that is why you wanted to talk with them.
- Commend them for their ambition in seeking a higher position. Ask for suggestions that would help them get by any awkwardness.
- Refuse to defend yourself or debate them if the conversation turns in that direction. You already have the position, so don't belittle yourself by defending your boss's decision. That is not your role.
- Avoid any performance management. This is not the time to talk to them about their development needs. If they have performance achievements or behavioral traits that are worth commending, do so with moderation.
- Lay out your expectations for your relationship going forward and reemphasize your willingness to be accessible.

3. *Hold a candid conversation with your best friend.* It is possible that your best friend will now be your employee. This is a challenge that new leaders often fail to fully consider. Favoritism, or even the perception of favoritism, can egregiously damage trust. It is like a parent trying to coach her child on a sports team. Either she displays favoritism, or she goes the opposite direction and turns unduly harsh. It is very difficult to be entirely objective. Even if you are, just the perception of favoritism can damage your launch.

    It is usually best to let your friend know that there will be changes. Let them know that the friendship is important, but the new relationship will require changes, or you would be neglecting your responsibilities. There will be times when the responsibilities of supervising take priority over the roles of friendship. Let them know that if the roles were reversed, you would expect the same of them.

4. *Solicit feedback from your team.* Develop a routine of getting feedback from your team on their perception of your leadership. It is especially important to do it early on. You don't want to launch your culture and then be oblivious as to how your team perceives your leadership. Here is a great tool to use: Periodically hand out three Post-it Notes at the end of a meeting. Ask them to complete three sentences in sixty seconds. The size of the Post-it Notes and the time constraint will prevent them from writing a PhD dissertation on all of your failures, and it will quickly surface the single most important point for each statement. This tool can be very helpful in launching a culture.

- Please start _______________________________
- Please stop _______________________________
- Please continue _______________________________

5. *Establish a peer network.* Build a networking group. Identify other leaders that you can be open with. Here are some vetting criteria for your networking candidates:
   - Multiple levels on the org chart. Include people that are facing some of the challenges that you presently face but also include more seasoned leaders. You want to hear "Been there, done that" on occasion.
   - Multiple organizations. You want to speak freely, so avoid someone in your department or organization, where this could be compromised.
   - Multiple sectors. Cross-pollinate ideas and solutions using leaders from the public, private, academic, NGO, athletic, military, or religious sectors.
   - Multiple generations. Tomorrow's leaders must become more effective at multi-generational leadership than today's leaders are. This is a great place to start.

6. *Err on the side of structure.* My dad was a high school teacher for many years. He saw that some of the young teachers came in fresh from college with only a four-year age advantage over their students. He observed that some teachers were determined to be liked, but developed difficulty in tightening up the structure once they realized that their control had been compromised. However, the teacher who came in with a tighter approach was able to loosen the structure in time as the culture developed.

PEER-LEADER QUOTE

Tomorrow's leader is one who empathically leads/advises and is not afraid to show humility towards subordinates at the appropriate times.

DANNY W. WHITE, CIV, DAF
Chief, Education Operations Branch
Air Force Special Operations Command
A1KE

Paradigm Shift

Some leaders never fully make this shift. Before you are in leadership, you are valued, recognized, compensated, and even promoted based on the job that *you* do. However, when you are in leadership, that type of evaluation ends! Now you will be valued, recognized, compensated, and even promoted based on the job that *others* do.

You see, in the work environment, senior management looks for the employee who manages their work well—they utilize resources well, they solve their own problems, and they achieve a desired outcome. So, senior management promotes them. The assumption is that if a person can manage their work well, then they should be able to manage other workers well. However, these skills are not synonymous.

Consider the NFL. Think of the long list of NFL Hall of Fame players that went on to become Hall of Fame coaches. OK, it isn't long. In fact, it's almost non-existent. There may be some Chicago Bears fans out there who want to debate, but regardless, it's a very short list. Occasionally you have that great field general take a coaching position. Rarely does that coaching career end well. On the other hand, you look at a great Hall of Fame coach and he may have played a few years as a backup safety; you can't recall hearing his name when he was playing.

Work on your paradigm shift. Employee development is a cornerstone of your future as a leader. All good leaders are good teachers.

Performance Management

If employment development is a cornerstone of your future success, how do you address underperforming employees? How are you going to do it? What is your strategy for identifying root causes of underperformance?

Here is what I would encourage you to do. Use what I call the **ASK PM Approach.** Don't forget this! If you forget everything else I say, don't forget this! Tattoo it on the back of your hand. OK, maybe not, but remember it. There are only three root causes for underperformance. Your task as a supervisor is to uncover and address that root cause. I call it the **ASK PM Approach:** *Attitude, Skill,* or *Knowledge.* Free InsideOutLeadership tip: the **ASK PM Approach** is just as applicable for your kids as it is for your employees. Take a moment and check out Exhibit 4. 1. and then let's explore it.

Don't Know: Information: If your employee is underperforming, then start questioning the **K**nowledge piece. Do they know *what* they are supposed to be doing? Do they understand their job description? Was your delegation clear? Did they understand when it was due? All of these issues will be solved with additional or clearer information.

Exhibit 4. 1.

ASK PM (Performance Management) Approach

Employee Problem	Leadership Solution
1. **Don't Know** (Knowledge)	<u>Information</u> (better job description, clearer delegation, etc.)
2. **Can't Do** (Skill)	<u>Instruction</u> (training, coaching, mentoring, etc.)
3. **Won't Do** (Attitude)	<u>Motivation</u> (carrot or the stick)

Can't Do: Instruction: If your employee is still underperforming after he or she understands *what* is expected, then you go to the second step. Do they *know* how to do it? This is a skill-targeted question. I am not asking if they went through the training; I am asking if they know *how* to do it. As hard as it is for a trainer to admit, there is a rumor that not everyone who goes through a skill-based training actually learns that particular skill. You may have to ask some probing questions and invest additional effort in monitoring.

Won't Do: Attitude: This is where it gets tricky. If your employee understands *what* (**K**nowledge) he or she is to do, and they know *how* (**S**kill) to do it, yet they are still underperforming, then there is only one option left: *Won't Do:* **A**ttitude. (How to motivate will be addressed in chapter 10.)

Just a caution: Many new bosses tend to assume that their underperforming employee's issue is *Won't Do*—which is attitude. They go straight to number three. Make a point of always starting at the top and working your way down. Keep in mind that none of these performance issues will be solved by either of the other two solutions. If an employee doesn't understand *what* (**K**nowledge) they are supposed to do, then no amount of training and motivating will ever work. If an employee doesn't know *how* (**S**kill) to do it, then no amount of information or motivation will ever work. And if they *won't* (**A**ttitude) do it, then no amount of information or instruction will work.

OK, one more caution: Be careful not to react to an employee's reaction (more about this in chapter 14). A colleague of mine worked his way through college by erecting these round metal grain bins that are scattered across the country. He worked for an excellent foreman who ran a year-round crew. One summer, corporate brought the foreman into the office and informed him that he was going to have to learn a new process for erecting these bins, and that as foreman he would be required to train the crew. He declined. They were mildly surprised, for he had always been cooperative. They emphasized that a new vendor had been secured and therefore a new erection process would be required. Again, he persistently refused. Finally, they told him that they would give him a bonus for the additional time and effort that would be required to train the crew. He stood up and said, "You can fire me, but I'm not doing it," and he walked out the door. They were stunned.

Suppose you were there in that office that day. What would you have thought of that foreman's performance? You might have thought that you know attitude when you see attitude, and that was definitely attitude. Don't react to reactions. Later in the day the foreman confided in my colleague, "I can't read." Suddenly, it became obvious that it was not an attitude problem—it was a skill problem. Reading is a skill. If they would have taken the time to use the **ASK PM Approach**, they very well may have uncovered the root problem. Always start at the top and work down.

Did I mention that it works with your kids too?

Summary—Here are the building blocks and best practices that will prepare you for tomorrow's leadership challenges.

- Work on your paradigm shift. You will now be recognized, paid, and promoted on the basis of the job that others do, rather than just the job that you do.
- Analyze your effectiveness in addressing unacceptable behavior. Remember, silence on your part in the face of unacceptable behavior will be perceived as approval.
- Prepare candid conversations with your team, competitor, and best friend when your next promotion occurs.
- Choose an opportunity in the near future to implement the brief feedback tool of please start, please stop, and please continue.
- Start your peer networking list today and take ownership for its launch.
- Teach the **ASK PM Approach** (see Exhibit 4. 1.) to a colleague to help solidify it in your mind.

CHAPTER 5

Life Lesson from a Flight Instructor

Precisely navigating with an unreliable compass.

It is an ironic habit of human beings to run faster
when they have lost their way.
—ROLLO MAY

You have seen him. It's sad. He starts his career strong and then fizzles when he approaches retirement.

I have watched several careers take off through the years that eventually flamed out. They quit their job…but still go to work. Here is how the downward spiral often goes. They start with enthusiasm, but the enthusiasm turns into frustration. The frustration, in time, turns into anger. The anger then turns them into an angry person. (There is a significant difference between a person who is angry and an angry person.) The anger within that angry person turns into apathy, and apathy turns into cynicism. All too frequently, they slide toward retirement and lose their health. It doesn't have to be this way!

The secret is this. Form the picture of your eight-to-five work life from the perspective of your 24/7 life, rather than the other way around. Here is what I mean. Work can be difficult and frustrating. In fact, it can beat you down over time. If you allow it to, work will form your view of your life. It can stress you out, make you irritable, apathetic, and withdrawn. Many have resorted to medications, prescribed and otherwise. Americans take more anxiety-related medications than do people in any other country in the world.[1]

You need to establish and maintain a strong life perspective and then take that perspective to work with you. Don't let work reshape your life perspective. Every day before you go to work, reboot. Every day, step back and form your fresh view of work from your life's perspective.

Need some help? Here we go. Do you realize that you live in the absolute Disneyland of human history? Seriously! If you made $34,200 in 2018, then you, my friend, are in the upper 1 percent-of the world's population.[2] You heard me. One percent! That means that 99 percent of the world's population would love to have your job on your worst day. If you took the average annual income of a US family of four that lives at or below the poverty line and made them a country unto themselves, they would be the thirty-first wealthiest country in the world out of 195 countries.[3] The average new US home in 2015 was 2,687 square feet[4] and the average new UK home was 968 square feet.[5]

You want more? More people will eat their dinner tonight with chopsticks than with metal utensils, and more people will eat their dinner tonight with their fingers than with chopsticks. We are the first culture in recorded history in which the major health challenges among those below the poverty line are obesity and obesity-related diseases.

Yet, when we go to work, we moan and we groan, we whine, and we complain. Many of us are untethered from the reality of the world in which we live.

When I travel abroad, I like to ask people what they think of Americans. Typically, their answers range from *pill-poppers* to *brash* to *wealthy* to *patriotic/nationalistic* to *mannerly*. In recent years I've been hearing a new one—*complainers*. They have a point. When you land in the States after having traveled abroad, you can tell that you are back home because you hear whining and complaining all around you.

Complaining has become America's second language, and complaining is the language of the victim. None of us wants to follow a victim; we want to follow overcomers. Remember the words of General Powell, "No matter how cold it is, you must never look cold. No matter how hungry you all are, you must never appear hungry. No matter how terrified you are, you must never look terrified. Because if you are scared, terrified, hungry, and cold, they will be scared, terrified, hungry, and." You cannot influence unless you have the courage to be different.

What is going on? We as Americans tend to view ourselves through the lens of work. We gain personal value from work. Think about this. How long do you go in a conversation with a stranger before you ask, or are asked, "What do you do for a living?" It's usually one of the first questions asked. Work should contribute value to our lives, but it should not define the value of our life. You need to tether to something beyond work, or work will distort your perspective on life.

Magnetic Compass or Directional Gyro

Forty-some years ago I stepped into a little Cessna 150 and slipped the surly bonds of earth at Sky Harbor International Airport in Phoenix, AZ. Life has never been the same. I went on to become a private pilot, instrument pilot, commercial pilot, and finally, an FAA-certified flight instrument instructor.

One of the primary navigational instruments that a pilot learns to use is the compass. Interestingly, most planes have at least two primary compasses. There is a separate need and use for each one. Here is how they work. Now, stay with me.

Heading Indicator (Directional Gyro or DG) This is your primary compass to maneuver the aircraft. This is the one that you use to turn to a specific heading, and it's relatively easy to maneuver with. It's usually electrically powered, and it operates off of an internal gyroscope. It's a smooth and steady instrument. However, it has one significant weakness that can prove to be deadly. The gyro is imperfect and will slowly retard over time, for reasons that would probably bore you if I took the time to explain. It can be very deceitful because you cannot determine that the instrument has become unreliable simply by looking at it. It's possible for you to be flying precisely on course according to your DG, but in reality, you may be substantially off course.

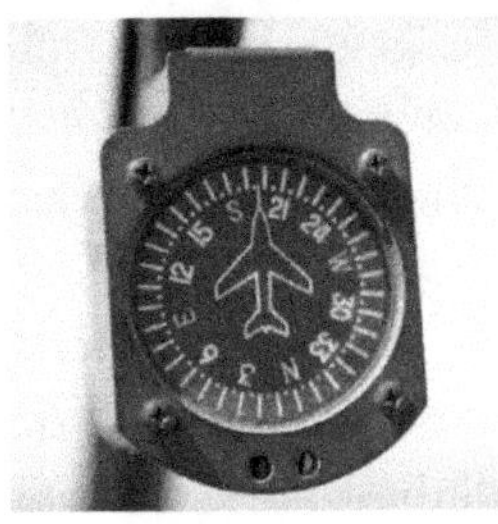

Magnetic Compass (Wet Compass) The Magnetic Compass, on the other hand, usually sits in a container of kerosene or mineral spirits and is one of the most reliable navigational instruments in the aircraft. It's basic. It simply picks up magnetic north which is obviously outside of the aircraft. Although it's reliable, it's almost impossible to maneuver with. It's quite unstable in turns, and it will oscillate back and forth once you roll out of your turn. These oscillations will decrease over several seconds, but they make it very difficult to precisely maneuver with. It will always, over time, reliably return to indicate your actual heading once you return to straight and level flight.

So, if the Magnetic Compass is reliable to navigate with, but unreliable to maneuver with, and the DG is reliable to maneuver with, but unreliable to navigate with, what then is the solution? The solution is to manually reset your DG to line up with the Magnetic Compass every fifteen minutes or so, but only when you are in straight and level flight. Resetting your DG to your Magnetic Compass provides you with reliable flight data that you can use to both navigate and maneuver.

Every day, we need to regularly reset our work-DG to align with our life-Magnetic Compass, which provides us with the data that enables us to both navigate and maneuver. Failure to regularly reset will cause us to get off track, and we may not even be aware of it!

PEER-LEADER QUOTE

I close the day with the following question under my desk
pad; would the following have been proud of me today?
Son, Wife, Parents, God? My response helps me refocus
for the next day.

MARK PEIFFER
Senior Vice President and Chief Financial Officer
Des Moines University

Life to Work Perspective

Now for the big question: What is life's tether? What is it that should give us a solid life perspective? How can we reset our work-compass to our life-compass?

Here is how I see it. We all know the pessimist, and he often gets a bum rap. But we need pessimists. In aviation, the optimist designed the airplane, but the pessimist designed the parachute. They do a great job of looking at the backside of a question. Granted, they're not always fun to work with, but we need them. However, they're not necessarily Negativists. All Negativists are pessimists but not all pessimists are Negativists.

Picture your work team. A work team is often comprised of three different types of people. You have the Negativists, the Positivists, and the Influenceables. (OK, none of these are actual words, I just made them up...but they are spelled correctly!) Your team may consist, on average, of about 10 percent Negativists, 10 percent Positivists, and 80 percent Influenceables. These percentages can shift significantly depending on a number of variables, not the least of which is the ability to hire and fire.

Now let's probe this.

- Do the Positivists influence the team? Sure.
- Do the Negativists influence the team? Sure.
- Which of the two, Positivists or Negativists, influences the team the most? Rarely does anyone ever suggest that Positivists influence a team more than Negativists. (See Exhibit 5. 1.) This means that if you as a team leader do not take appropriate actions, then over time your team will inevitably become more negative in its outlook.

Exhibit 5. 1.

Life-Work Perspectives

- What are the traits of a Negativist and how do I recognize them?
   o With each of your initiatives, you feel like you are pushing a square ball. There is resistance at almost every step.
   o When the Negativist is absent from the meeting, the atmosphere is different. When they are on vacation, the work culture is lighter and less restrained. (Remember Rick?)
   o They are herd animals. If you find one, then you usually find more than one. If you have ever worked with teenagers, then you know what I'm talking about. Suppose you are at a teen party and you physically

position yourself where you can watch this new culture start to develop. Depending on the size of the group, in about fifteen minutes the Negativists will find each other. They can pick up the vibes. This information becomes critical when you have two or more on your team. You want to minimize the negative synergy using separation. Put one in this corner of the room and the other in that corner. Put one on first shift and the other on second shift. Put one on first lunch and the other on second lunch. Be careful about putting more than one on a project team.

o   When you walk into the presence of a Negativist and then walk out, you are always less than when you started. (See Exhibit 5. 2. below.) They steal from you. You walk away from their presence frustrated, distracted, discouraged, angry, stymied…you get the picture. You leave diminished. Curiously, most Negativists are oblivious as to the extent of their negative influence. When you walk into the presence of an Influenceable, you walk away unchanged for the most part. However, when you walk away from the presence of a Positivist, you are more invigorated, determined, informed, encouraged, creative, tenacious, and energized. (See Exhibit 5. 2.)

Exhibit 5. 2.

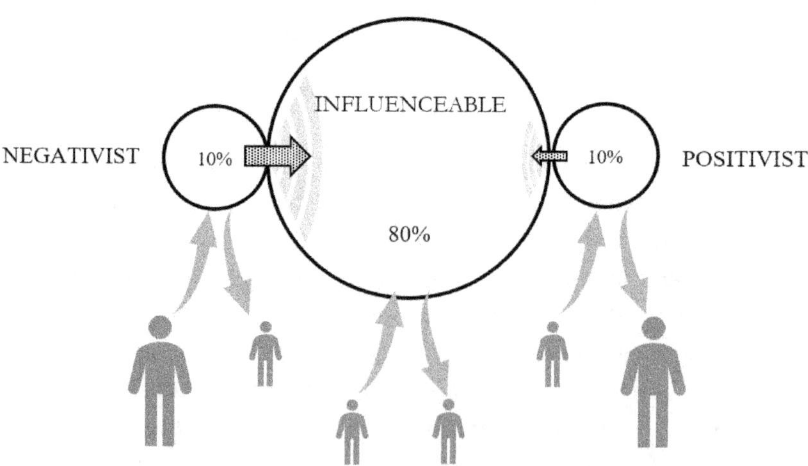

- The Positivist believes that life just can't get any better, while the Negativist fears the same.
- Now for the drum roll. **Why?**

It is not infrequent that a young, optimistic team leader steps into their new position and sets their performance-management sights on the Negativist. They are determined to see that Negativist move into the ranks of the Influenceable, if not the ranks of the Positivist. However, they often end up discouraged after spending a disproportionate amount of leadership-stamina on the project. There are some people that the team leader simply *cannot* change. Don't misunderstand me—I am one of those people who believe that everyone can change. I just don't believe that the team leader can change everyone. With that logic, even Jesus had a sketchy record with some team members.

The reason the Negativist is a Negativist is because of their life perspective. Every place that life has touched them, it has *stolen* from them. They got the fuzzy end of the lollipop in life. They should have had better parents, better siblings, a better house, better coach, better friends, better schools, better teachers, better car, better education, better looks, better country, better job, better spouse, better kids, better... They look at life as though it is a *THIEF*. (See Exhibit 5. 3.)

The reason the Positivist is a Positivist is *also* because of their life perspective. Every place that life has touched them, it has *given* to them. They see life as a gift. They don't feel that they deserve the parents and siblings that they have, or the house, coach, friends, schools, teachers, cars, education, looks, country, job, spouse, kids, etc. Every day they reset their life-compass and remind themselves of how life has undeservedly privileged them. Life is a *GIFT*.

Both of my boys, Jeremy and Nathan, are also pilots. If one day they piled up the plane on the side of a mountain, I don't know how I would face the next day. But I wouldn't have the luxury of bitterness because I didn't deserve them in the first place. If I get terminal cancer this year, I wouldn't have the luxury of bitterness because I didn't deserve these many years of life in the first place. Every stolen item in the list of the Negativist, and every gifted item in the list of the Positivist, has a shelf life. They will all come to an end. They are only temporarily on loan.

Do you sense the irony here? Everyone that comes into the presence of the Negativist gets *robbed*, although the Negativist sees life as a *thief*. Everyone that comes into the presence of the Positivist *receives*, although the Positivist sees life as a *gift*.

Exhibit 5. 3.

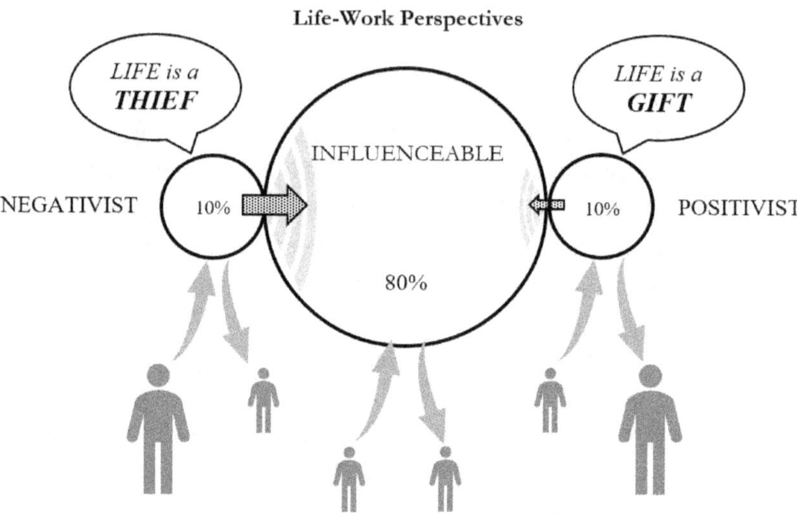

If the leader can't change the Negativist, yet everybody can change, how then can the Negativist change? It isn't by acquiring more of life's gifts. Think about it. Some Negativists were born with a silver spoon in their mouth. One's perspective on life doesn't change when more gifts are added. In fact, I have a friend who used to be a poster child for the Negativist and is now a poster child for the Positivist. What initiated the change? He was in an accident and lost the ability to walk. Life "stole" from him, which caused him to reset and realize the value of life and its gifts. Negativists can be transformed into Positivists when they come to a personal reckoning with their own existential tether to significance.

You are much more likely to have a strong career when you can still savor life even in the midst of the darkest days at work.

Summary—Here are the building blocks and best practices that will prepare you for tomorrow's leadership challenges.

- Reset your life's Directional Gyro by establishing a daily reboot. Approach each day by mentally reviewing the bigger picture of your life.
- Listen to yourself talk. What percentage of your unguarded conversation consists of complaining? Remember, complaining is the language of the victim.
- Identify a trusted peer who you can openly vent with.

- Memorize some gratitude distractors that will enable you to massage a complaining conversation in another direction. "Sure, work can seem unfair but overall we really have it good because…"
- Develop tactics to manage your Negativists.
- Set a personal goal to leave everyone that you come in contact with better off than they were when they came. Premeditate the gifts you will leave them like encouragement, knowledge, compassion, empathy, listening, support, direction, correction, etc.

CHAPTER 6

Embracing Change, and Tradition

> When the world changes faster than
> species can adapt, many fall out.
> This is the case whether the agent drops
> from the sky in a fiery streak
> or drives to work in a Honda.
> —Elizabeth Kolbert

Not again! You just finished learning the latest and greatest software system and now they're going to exchange it for a new one. Again. Really?

Who in the US workforce cannot identify with that statement, regardless of whether they use a software system or not? Senior management is perpetually trying to make the work environment lean and mean, but to the employee it often feels vicious and anorexic.

And then the questions begin to fly:

Didn't we just change it?
What was wrong with this system?

Whose idea was this anyway?
Do they really think we are going to buy into this?

There are few words that are more volatile in the workplace today than the word *change*. It stimulates strong emotions, and often, resistance.

Here is an exercise for you. Clasp your hands together by intertwining your fingers, like in this picture. (It may be prudent to delay this if you are listening to the audio book while driving.) Now look at the position of your thumbs. Which thumb is on top? Do you realize that approximately 50% of the population places the opposite thumb on top? It has nothing to do with whether you are left- or right-handed. Now, reverse it all the way down. Unclasp your fingers and re-clasp them so that your opposite thumb is on top. Does that feel weird, or what? Do you realize that approximately 50% of the people around you think this is normal? Now, go back to the way you clasped your hands the first time. Normal feels good, doesn't it?

Try this. Fold your arms like the lady in the picture. Which arm is on top? It may or may not be the same side as the thumb you preferred in the last activity. Now reverse it. Put the opposite arm on top. Does that feel weird? Again, about 50% of the population places the opposite arm on top. Now return your arms to your *normal* position. Normal is so wonderful!

So, why do those ways feel so normal? The answer is simple. One time when we were toddlers, we first clasped our hands, or folded our arms, in those same positions. The rest is history.

The seven words of a dying career are *"I've always done it that way before."* Accepting change is quite challenging for some of us. The leaders of tomorrow will be required to lead reluctant people through change. The place to begin is by getting on top of our own reluctance to change. My financial retirement plan would be much more robust if I got a nickel every time I heard the argument, "You can't teach an old dog new tricks." I agree with the phrase except for two things: these are not new tricks and you are not an old dog. Other than that, I agree with it.

It can be so subtle. I've watched as good people hit a plateau in their life or career, and subconsciously kick in their cruise control. It's subtle and it can be very seductive. The more life we process, the more change-acceptance falls on our volition. That means we must deliberately make that choice to consider embracing that change.

PEER-LEADER QUOTE

Tomorrow's leader is one who embraces
and inspires innovative solutions.

LANATTA R. CLARK, MSN, RN,
Chief Organizational Development
Department of Veterans Affairs

It's a mindset. A mammal reaches full physical maturation early on in its existence. Human beings, for instance, reach full physical maturation somewhere around eighteen to twenty-five years of age, even though we may live to be one hundred. Most reptiles, on the other hand, literally grow until the day they die. Tomorrow's leader needs to have a reptilian mindset. Here are some stretching tips to get you nimbler.

1. Talk to yourself.
   - What is the worst that can happen?
   - What change in my past did I initially reject, but later embraced, and today I am so glad that I did?
   - Why, specifically, am I reluctant to embrace this change? (fear, laziness, disbelief, etc.)
   - What potential benefits may come from this change?
   - How will my leadership impact be affected if I embrace this change? If I reject this change?
2. Build change habits into your life.
   - Go to a different restaurant.
   - Order different food.
   - Drive home a different way.
   - Vacation in a different place.
   - Listen to an opposing political view without trying to debate or correct.
3. Reward yourself when you embrace a frustrating change.

Rate of Change

Now let's pause for a moment. Let's stop thinking about change and momentarily think about the *rate* of change. My parents are in their mid-nineties and still live alone. Occasionally, in the midst of a conversation, I will have a mind-boggling awareness: "You were alive when…Civil War veterans walked the earth…Charles Lindbergh crossed the Atlantic…Wyatt Earp was still around!"

It is crazy to think what the eyes of those who lived predominantly in the twentieth century saw. Let's get crazy. Think about what the world was like at the turn of the twentieth century.

What was the main means of transportation? Horse, buggy, cart, wagon, and walking.

What fuel did they heat their homes with? Wood and coal.

What fuel did they use to cook their food? Wood and coal.

What fuel did they use to light their houses? Kerosene and candles.

Where did they go to the bathroom? Outside and in outhouses.

Chew on this. The world at the beginning of the twentieth century was closer to the world of two thousand years ago than it is to the world of today. The citizen of the twentieth century personally absorbed more change than the collective generations of two thousand years! It is doubtful to me that this world will ever ask one generation to absorb more change in one lifetime than the life lived in the twentieth century. I believe that change will continue to escalate, possibly exponentially. But the twentieth century took us from antiquity to the heights of technology.

A word to the Ys and Zs: It may appear that the older generation is firmly entrenched in their lounge chairs of life, but that may not be the case. Start by considering how much change they have observed. It isn't that older people don't know anything about change, it's that they typically suffer from change saturation. Understanding this may help you lead older employees through change.

Tradition – Rescuing the Baby from the Bath Water

Caution! Change is not synonymous with progress. This statement may startle some people, but change can inadvertently lead to regression. It is possible, in our quest to worship at the altar of change, that we may be sacrificing valuable traditions that tomorrow we may regret. Wisdom-driven reluctance is healthy for tomorrow's leaders. It is best not to tear down a specific wall of tradition until we have a full grasp of what that wall was protecting us from. (More about this in chapter 19.) Writer G. K. Chesterton said it best: "Tradition means giving votes to the most obscure of all classes, our ancestors. It is the democracy of the dead."[1]

Changing at the "Rate of Sloth"

One of the more common responses from some of the leaders in my classes at the Federal Executive Institute is the belief that the federal government is incapable of changing, or if it does, it is at the "rate of sloth." This sentiment is not without evidence.

Public sector organizations generally have a fundamentally opposite purpose for existing than do private sector organizations. Public organizations *utilize* funds to provide goods and services, while private sector organizations manufacture goods and services to *acquire* funds. This essential distinction wafts through organizations and displays itself in different ways. One of these is in the rate of change. Public sector organizations are more stable and predictable, while private sector organizations have the luxury of experimentation.

If you are in the government sector, then let me encourage you about your future. When I first started teaching leaders in the federal sector many years ago, there were still a few of the Greatest Generation in the workforce. I explained to them that an entirely new hoard of workers, called Generation X, was on the doorstep, and there would be significant changes ahead. This generation, I explained, would not put up with working sixty hours a week, including weekends. They were not going to forgo their vacations. They wanted to take time off for their kids' Little League games. They wanted a balanced life.

Skepticism abounded. I heard things like, "They are to come to work when we need them, and they are to work when they are at work. It is called *work*. Can you see the correlation?" Today we have the phrase *work-life balance* on the tip of our tongues, solely because a large segment of the workforce put their Gen Xer foot down. To this day, almost every organization, public or private, has this phrase in its vocabulary and probably in its policy book. Congress has made laws to support work-life balance. Even bathrooms are designed differently because of work-life balance. We now have changing stations in men's bathrooms.

The change that Generation Y (millennials) will make in the workplace won't take nearly as long as the work-life change took with Generation X. Hang on. I think I hear Bob Dylan again...

Shifting Labor Values

So, change is coming, and you need to be prepared. What will this change look like? In his best seller *A Whole New Mind: Why Right-Brainers Will Rule the Future*, Daniel H. Pink argues that we are on the cusp of a new paradigm on how we value labor in the workforce. It goes something like this.

First paradigm shift: Mechanized Age. Let's head back to the turn of the twentieth century. Paul Bunyan with his big biceps and his big axe was chopping away in northern Minnesota. Poor little Bob, with his puny little biceps and his pathetic little axe, was also chipping away. Culture's value obviously flowed toward Paul. Because he could fell far more trees than little Bob, he received more recognition, opportunities, compensation, security, and promotions than little Bob did.

But then one day a machine was developed that replaced the axe, and the machine was one that Bob could master. He could now fell far more trees than Paul. The Mechanized Age had arrived. In a short period of time, the cultural value of labor shifted away from the Pauls to the Bobs. Now Bob was receiving more recognition, opportunities, compensation, security, and promotions than Paul was. This put the Pauls in a quandary. Some Pauls saw what was coming, bit the bullet, accepted the change, and learned how to run the machine. However, some Pauls locked themselves into the seven words of a dying career and chopped their way into oblivion.

Second paradigm shift: Information Age. The second of three paradigm shifts occurred in the 1960s. It is possible that the decade of the sixties was the decade we saw the most scientific advancements of the twentieth century. I'm an old-enough geezer to remember when the first digital pocket calculators came out. Before that, the adding machines and typewriters were manual and emitted clack-clack sounds every time keys were pressed. Then out came these fancy pocket calculators. They had a window at the top with lit numbers and when you pressed a key, the corresponding number appeared in the window. You could press 2 + 2 =, and instantaneously see the answer 4 appear in the window. It was wild.

NASA engineers were working feverishly at the time to meet JFK's challenge to put a man on the moon by the end of the decade. These brilliant engineers walked around with a slide rule in their pocket and would periodically take it out and wield their mathematical wonders. Then, in walked these young scientists with their freshly printed diplomas and their fancy new calculators. They began to run mathematical circles around these NASA engineers. Once again, the flow of cultural value began to shift from the mechanized to the digital. Once again, decisions had to be made. Some NASA engineers saw what was coming, bit the bullet, accepted the change, and learned the new technology. However, some engineers embraced the seven words of a dying career and slid their way into oblivion.

<u>Third paradigm shift: Conceptual Age</u>. Today we are on the cusp of a third paradigm shift called the Conceptual Age. Here is how this works. Technology, of course, will continue to develop. However, we are discovering that, as technology has been rising there has been a parallel decline in personal meaning. An alarming decline. The increased suicide rate among teens ought to be on the front page of every newspaper. People sense that while we're impressing ourselves with the development of technology, meaning seems to be seeping out of the cracks of society.

Let me be clear. I am no Luddite. I like the latest GPS, smart phone, Surface, etc. But the word *technology* itself should give us a hint of its limitations. Technology comes from the root word *technique*, and the word *technique* is a process word. It's a "how-to" word. Technology enables us to communicate with more people today faster than ever before, but it doesn't help us at all with what we should say or write of significance. Technology enables us to fly more people to Beijing, and faster, but it doesn't help us at all with why we should go or what we should do there of meaning. Technology's territory is the "how-to" but not the "why-to." Nietzsche told us, "He who has a *why* to live can bear almost any *how*."[2] As we are grabbing increasingly greater handfuls of the *how*, the sands of the *why* have been seeping out between our fingers.

Enter the Conceptual Age. Technology will continue to expand, but our awareness is growing that it is simply not delivering on meaning. This is where your golden opportunity as a leader comes in. Your opportunity is: Build tethers to significance. Here is one way that will take shape. We used to teach physicians how to have good bedside manners, and lawyers how to have good persuasion skills, and IT SMEs to have good customer-service skills. Today the emphasis is starting to shift. Now we are looking for people who have great bedside manners who are physicians, and people who can empathetically persuade who also have law degrees, and people who prefer others who are IT SMEs. Remember this—"Millennials don't quit jobs, they quit people."

Summary—Here are the building blocks and best practices that will prepare you for tomorrow's leadership challenges.

- Choose silence as your first response the next time you face an undesirable change.
- Memorize your personal list of self-questions to use when the really difficult change rears its ugly head.

- Create a habit of breaking a habit. Eat a different restaurant, drive home a different way, prepare a new dish, watch a different genre of docuseries, make a new friend, etc.
- Ask a trusted colleague if they see you more as a reptile or as a mammal. (You may want to explain these first!)

CHAPTER 7

A Seminal Career Tip: Leading Change

Leveraging the power of the first follower.

Without deviation from the norm, progress is not possible.
—FRANK ZAPPA

t's one thing to be open to change personally, but it's an entirely different animal to successfully lead change in a change-reluctant culture. However, that is exactly what tomorrow's leaders will be asked to do. Tomorrow's mantra is "Get more done, get it done faster, and with fewer resources."

Position yourself at the starting line by understanding that there are two perspectives on change. Senior leaders view change from an entirely different perspective than that of the frontline employee. Check out these different perspectives in Exhibit 7. 1.

Exhibit 7. 1.

Change Perspective

<u>Senior Leader</u>	<u>Employee</u>
Career security	Career insecurity
Leadership	Victimized
Progress	Regression
Just business	Personal

If you fall somewhere between the senior leader and the employee on the org chart, then your task is to implement the change and make both parties happy. Good luck with this one.

Reluctance to Change

Actually, if you are going to build tethers to significance, then you need more than just luck. You need to understand *why* people are reluctant to change. The most common cause that I hear for failing to accept change is fear. However, some people simply think the change idea is stupid, or a flavor of the month, or a public spectacle, or a boss's personal vendetta against a previous boss, and nothing more. Change reluctance is a complex subject which we don't have the time and space to deeply explore here, but we can examine the most common cause, and that is fear. But just being aware that fear causes reluctance to change doesn't go very far because there are very different fears that the leader needs to understand in order to construct tethers to significance. Here are three common fears that drive change reluctance.

1. <u>Fear of failure</u>: Hovering in the back of our insecure minds is this annoying reality that I may not be up to the task. I may not be able to do the job required to embrace and implement the change. This fear may be harbored in skill deficiency, time constraints, or relationship challenges. Regardless, the outcome of the fear of failure remains the same.

    To construct tethers to significance, you need to understand what that failure translates into in the life of your employee. That employee, when faced with this daunting change, is thinking things like: "What will it be like when I fail in front of my boss and colleagues? Will I get demoted or even lose my job? What will I tell my family? Will I lose my car? What will I tell my neighbor? What will Thanksgiving dinner be like?"

Caution: This individual will most likely show their fear by reacting in *anger* to a change. You may hear things like, "Whose dumb idea was this anyhow? Now they expect us to do this?" Avoid reacting to their reaction. If you listen carefully, you can hear fear whispering behind the anger. Address the fear of failure rather than the anger and you will start constructing a fresh tether to significance.

2. <u>Fear of the unknown</u>: This is a perplexing fear that I see some leaders inadvertently misread. For the adventurous spirit, the unknown is enticement. To many people, the unknown can be a lonely terror.

    Early in my career I was a counselor and occasionally dealt with domestic abuse cases. Usually it was a woman who was battered by a spouse or partner. We would remove her from the house of horror and provide her with safety and resources. We perceived these efforts to be a great launch pad for her new future. But all too frequently, she chose to return to the house of horror rather than to face the silent terror of the unknown.

    Caution: It usually takes more than simply providing the resources necessary for change implementation for their fear to subside. It will require more listening, more engagement, and more recognition. The pain of remaining the same needs to become greater than the fear of the unknown.

3. <u>Fear of success</u>: This might sound like an odd one, but it is not infrequently found. Here is how this works. They think, "If I buy into this, and it goes well, then they are going to expect more of me, and I don't need more."

    The effective change-leader not only understands that fear generates change-reluctance, but also understands the root cause of that fear. Your tethers to significance will look different for those who fear failure, for those who fear the unknown, and for those who fear success.

Leading Stupid Change Projects

If you have never been there before, it goes something like this. Your boss has just handed you a major change initiative with a pressing deadline. You have been tasked with leading it. It becomes readily apparent, after a brief review, that this plan would fit neatly into the rather large folder titled *Really Dumb Ideas*. You begin to feel the burden of rolling this out to your change-reluctant team, and then trying to lead them in a successful implementation of the change. What to do?

Conventional wisdom instructs us to bite the bullet, suck it up, and sell it. Fake it until you make it. Conventional wisdom often contains some valuable concepts, but all too frequently it contains misleading ideas as well. Let's sort them out. It's true that once you sign on the dotted line to become a leader, you represent the organization you work for. You are the face of that organization to your team, employees, and customers. It's also true that your opinions, at times, need to be subservient to a greater value. But you knew that. You have a responsibility to your boss and your organization to lead this change with your best efforts. And yet, your employees know when you're faking it, and it's hard to follow a faker. Thus, the change leader's conundrum.

Here is where you need to go.

1. <u>Search for value</u>: Re-review the change initiative. Are there any morsels of value that you can identify? Are there any ancillary morsels? Can you find anything in the process that will generate value and meaning, even if the initiative fails?

2. <u>Find the backstory</u>: Talk with your boss, or with those who have knowledge of the initiative, and respectfully probe for reasons. Expand your understanding of what generated the initiative and what problem(s) it hopes to solve.

3. <u>Share strategy</u>: Optimistically brainstorm strategies and tactics with your boss about how you can successfully implement the initiative. This step may stimulate some lipstick ideas for this ugly pig. It will also convey to your boss some of the challenges that you anticipate.

4. <u>Roll the initiative out to your team</u>: Objectively explain the change initiative to your team and then turn silent. Give your team time to vent. You had some time to absorb the news, so give them the same luxury. Don't try to prematurely convert them. Be patient and observant. If the conversational momentum continues to build in opposition to the initiative, it's time to step in and take control. However, if there are some signs of openness to the change, let the conversation continue. If there is a voice that even considers the possibility that the initiative may have some value, probe that voice with questions. Let the team know that that person's voice carries weight with you.

5. <u>Permanently delete the word *change* from your vocabulary</u>: Candidate Barack Obama ran on *hope and change*, which ignited a large segment of

You also want a digital-savvy team. Most Gen Xers and boomers are digital-immigrants, but most Gen Yers and Gen Zers are digital-natives. Leverage them.

- Rookies and veterans: Include people with a fresh perspective and people with organizational knowledge.

- Non-friends: Include people that are not on your birthday-card list. Remember, they move in, and influence, a circle of people that you probably don't.

- Naysayer: This may sound odd, but consider this. He will provide inside knowledge from the opposition. More importantly, if this person can be converted and become a supporter, he will carry substantial influence with other naysayers.

2. <u>Vision Clarification</u>: This is a big one. Articulate the vision using the nomenclature and terminology of those whom you most want to get on board. Remember, people don't buy into plans, they tether to vision. (Review chapter 3 to brush up on this.) Use your team to design and articulate the vision. The more they are engaged in constructing the vision, the more likely it will be that they will get on board. Anytime people voluntarily invest effort and energy in anything, their affections will follow their investment. Remember, the opposite of vision is not no-vision; it is division.

3. <u>Short-Term Success</u>: Remember, you are fighting for the bulk of the team. A great way to soften the voices of the naysayers and strengthen the voices of the first followers is to design your change-implementation plan to include STSs, or Short-Term Successes. If your plan does not provide for STSs, this can put your success in jeopardy. Silence will eventually embolden the naysayers and discourage the first followers. Early indicators of success will counter that silence. They give hope to the first followers, minimize the voice of the naysayers, and start to sway the bulk of the team that may still be on the fence.

4. <u>Communication Consistency</u>: "One-and-done" is not a good communication strategy. Keep your vision, plan, STSs, and updates before those who are affected by the change. A good approach is the 3x3x3 tool. Here is how it works. Suppose you have a fresh STS you want to communicate to the group at large (work group, department, division, organization).

- 3 People: Use three different people to communicate the STS. Avoid becoming the sole spokesman for the initiative. When possible, include former naysayers.

- 3 Communiqués: Have each of the three people communicate the STS three different times within a specified time frame. This could be a day, week, month, or quarter depending on the duration of the change initiative.

- 3 Venues: Have each of the three people use three different communication venues for each of their three different communiqués. This could be a report in a meeting, an email tag line, a voice mail, a poster, or an announcement. Don't forget the most important communication venue—the water cooler.

5. <u>Accountability Tools</u>: It's one thing to design a successful plan, but it's an entirely different matter to successfully implement one. If your role is restricted to designing the plan but not executing it, then you might want to refer to chapter 18 on Political Savvy.

   If you are involved in the execution phase, then consider the power of verbal consistency. People tend to follow through if they commit in a public manner.

   Here is an illustration of verbal consistency. For a few years I worked as a consultant with an academic institution that came into existence through a three-way merger. It was a great concept, but one that was fraught with challenges. Each of the merging entities had previously functioned independently, so there was understandable friction. I was tasked by the president of the institution with designing a strategic plan. For one year I sat down with a navigational team from the three previously independent entities and forged a strategic plan. It was rough sledding at first, but they persevered. The plan was well-thought-out and well-articulated. It was thorough and detailed; so much so that each point of the plan was supported by specific tasks and deadlines. Each task also included the name of a volunteer who was responsible for the execution of the task. The plan was well received by the president and the board. They asked me to stay on for another year to help execute the plan. We started off with enthusiasm, but it quickly vanished among the multitude of daily responsibilities. The volunteers meant well, but the follow-through often wasn't there. So, we created a website dedicated to the strategic plan that was available to all. It included the plan, tasks, deadlines, and most importantly, the name of the responsible volunteer. That changed everything. Once the name of the volunteer became public, verbal consistency took over. They did what they said they were going to do.

6. <u>Cultural Anchor</u>: Don't let your hard work go to waste. Are more changes coming? You bet. Use this specific change initiative to develop a change-receptive work culture. Develop your *Six-Step Change Leadership Plan* into a habit when approaching change. You can also use it as a mentoring tool for aspiring leaders. You will be glad someday that you took the extra effort to anchor change-receptivity into the fabric of your work culture.

Summary—Here are the building blocks and best practices that will prepare you for tomorrow's leadership challenges.

- Monitor a change-leader that you admire. When it comes to leading change, record what they do but that you don't. Integrate their actions into your leadership approach.
- Develop drilldown questions that will help you understand an employee's fear of change.
- Teach your team what professionalism actually is and then sprinkle the word into your everyday conversation.
- Look for an opportunity to execute the Six Step Change Leadership Plan.
- Identify and develop some potential first followers, and then strategically place them in greater areas of influence.
- Take ownership of a difficult change initiative that your boss wants implemented.

CHAPTER 8

Critical Thinking, or Lack Thereof

Thoughts on thinking.

Thinking is the hardest work there is,
which is probably the reason so few engage in it.
—Henry Ford

OK, this is the chapter where you may want to get a second caramel macchiato. It involves a little philosophy—but philosophy that is so relevant to your life and leadership. Grab a second venti. I will wait for you. You need to be at the top of your game for this one.

Critical thinking seems to be in its death throes. We can already see its replacements taking the field. Decisions are being made, problems are being solved, and lives are being planned on the basis of emotions, lazy thinking, group thinking, manipulation, deceit, and even default. This moves the critical thinkers to the sideline, and it moves the shouters, manipulators, name-callers, connivers, and deceivers to the first team.

Possibly the most daunting challenge for tomorrow's leader is learning how to successfully lead in a culture that has an increasingly subjective view of truth. Before we proceed, it is best that we come up with a working definition of truth. Truth as "that which conforms to reality" seems difficult to improve upon. Truth reflects that which is. It is a flawless verbal mirror of reality.

Consider the larger picture for a moment. You are an involuntary draftee in a daily battle. This battle rages on the personal level, familial level, work level, cultural level, and even world level. It is the ever-present battle between chaos and order. We all want order in our lives. We want to conduct our lives free of adversity. We want a clear and unimpeded career path. We want trustworthy relationships. We want to be healthy. We want our work environment to be meritocratic and predictable, we want the weather to be cooperative, and we want good to prevail on a global scale. But the reality is that chaos is persistent and often triumphant over order. Every person has a familial relationship that is wounded. Every person has a friend who has betrayed them. Every person knows someone who has faced an unfair and untimely death. Every person has a multitude of daily skirmishes with chaos, from flat tires to missed buses, contrarian waiters, narcissistic bosses, stolen bikes, disappointing family members, negative health news, and hail damage.

Here is your tether to significance: *Deceit is the language of chaos, and truth is the language of order*. When you have a proper relationship with truth, you advance not only the order in your small sphere of influence, but also the order of your surrounding culture. When deceit becomes the pattern, chaos is advanced even when there is a momentary benefit from the deceit. Many Americans, of all different political stripes, believe that US culture is becoming more chaotic. It is not coincidental that phrases depicting truth as elastic have become a part of our vocabulary. Can you say *alternative facts, spin, live your own truth, fake news*, etc.? Every time you tell the truth, you advance order, regardless of the momentary pain that truth-telling can bring. Every time you deceive, you advance chaos, regardless of the momentary benefit that deceit-telling can bring.

If you should go to Oslo, Norway, you will find a pedestrian bridge near the Norwegian Parliament with a sign that boldly proclaims, *Truth is Flexible*. It is a view that I do not share with my Norwegian ancestors. Truth exists independent of humanity. Once truth loses its independent objectivity, then the word *lie* will be removed from the dictionary. It will become obsolete, and truth will only be truth if so determined by those in power. Deceit cannot exist without a point of reference, and accountability dies when each person fully lives their "own truth." Verbal Photoshopping may be our culture's pattern; just don't make it yours.

Now I understand that we all make decisions based upon our own perspective. That is certainly true. But our own perspective is still our own opinion—it does not make it true. Everyone has a right to their own opinion and to express that opinion, but no one has a right to their own truth. My belief system does not affect the existence of truth. This timeless belief, that we can come together in reasoned agreement, is constructed on the assumed conviction that truth exists, and that truth often displays itself through evidence and facts. However, once truth becomes elastic, the critical-thinking funeral procession will begin. Most importantly, your life and your leadership will now become easily manipulatable. The plethora of new phrases regarding truth's 'elasticity' is not a good sign for the critical thinker.

Take the common phrase, "That is my reality." This statement indicates that this person is living in their own world regardless of external evidence and facts. Regardless of objective truth. Regardless of independent reality. Some may even suggest this is a step in the direction of delusion. If you push this thinking to the extreme, you may end up there. The *English-Oxford Living Dictionary* defines delusion as *"characterized by or holding idiosyncratic beliefs or impressions that are contradicted by reality or rational argument."* Critical thinking is ultimately dependent on the existence of objective truth.

It reminds me of an online article I read about a woman who went clothes shopping. She wore the same red dress to a variety of clothing stores, ranging from the bargain-basement type to the high-end stores that require an appointment. She stood in front of the mirror at each of the stores and took a picture of her reflection in their mirror. She then posted the pictures from the different stores online. Fascinating! The mirror in the bargain store showed her reflection as you would expect, completely accurate. However, her reflection in the high-end store showed her with a slimmer, more desirable figure. The mirror was intentionally altered in such a way that it would pleasantly deceive her about her appearance. She can stand in front of the high-end store's distorted mirror and declare that it is her truth; but that doesn't make it so. Truth is reality's bargain-basement mirror...and it is accurate.

Enemies of Critical Thinking

I didn't say *challenges* to critical thinking, or even the less acceptable *problems* to critical thinking. I said *enemies*. Tomorrow's leader will be contending with three enemies of critical thinking and they will be doing so even more than they do right now. What are these enemies?

<u>Lethargic Thinking</u>: It was Daniel Kahneman's best seller, *Thinking, Fast and Slow*, that so clearly articulated how we are becoming increasingly lethargic thinkers.[17] This Nobel Memorial Prize recipient thoroughly displays how we have come to rely on fast thinking and shun deep thinking—or as he calls it, slow thinking.

Herein lies a hidden opportunity. If you are willing to invest the time and effort to think deeply instead of being satisfied with the pat and quick answer, you will have an excellent future. For a great tethering question, consider using "To what end?" It takes more time to answer this question, and the answers may be annoying, but it stimulates a mildly skeptical approach which forces the current considerations at hand to be evaluated by the overall or long-term purpose.

To avoid lethargic thinking when it comes to problem solving, consider the *Five Levels of Why*.

Scenario: You walk into your office and discover your team sitting in a circle instead of working on their computers. You begin your inquiry.

1. *Why* aren't you working?
   Team answer: The computers are down.
2. *Why* are the computers down?
   Team answer: The electricity is off.
3. *Why* is the electricity off?
   Team answer: A breaker tripped.
4. *Why* did the breaker trip?
   Team answer: We installed computers on a serial circuit instead of a dedicated circuit.
5. *Why* did you install them on a serial circuit instead of a dedicated circuit?
   Team answer: Well it was Friday afternoon…

It is on the fourth or fifth level of *why* that you start to uncover the root problem. It is on the fifth level that you may hear answers that reveal a resource problem, a personnel problem, a training problem, a morale problem, or even a sabotage problem—none of which would be uncovered without taking the time to deeply inquire. If you as a leader develop the habit of solving the problem yourself after the second or third *why*, then you may find yourself to be a firefighter. You spend far too much of your time putting out fires instead of tenaciously pursuing the root cause.

Lethargic thinking is often displayed in a tendency to seek the minimal effort to deal with an issue instead of investing cognitive effort in attaching the issue to the overall purpose and value. Critical-thinking leaders of tomorrow must have the courage to preside over demise when deemed necessary.

<u>Biased Thinking</u>: Our intellectual hard drive is bent. We have cognitive biases that distort the way we see reality. These biases stand in the way of critical thinking. Here are your four basic cognitive biases.

- *The Bandwagon Bias*: The tendency to think or act in certain ways because other people do. We all feel it; whether it's trying to keep up with the Joneses, or the cultural intimidation to take a certain moral or political position. There are two ways the Bandwagon Bias confronts us.
  - o Abilene Paradox:[2] A group makes a collective decision that runs counter to the thoughts and opinions of the individuals within the group, but the individuals remain silent because they don't want to "rock the boat" and risk offense.
  - o Groupthink: A group makes a collective decision that runs counter to the thoughts and opinions of the individuals within the group, but the individuals *change* their thinking to conform to the collective decision. Although both the Abilene Paradox and Groupthink are influenced by the same forces, there is a distinction between the two. In the Abilene Paradox the team members don't change their view, they only pretend to. In Groupthink, the members actually start thinking alike. Either way, we all want to get along and be accepted, but leadership requires the thermostat mentality.
- *The Confirmation Bias*: The brain's inclination to seek out information that supports its own preconceived notions. We subconsciously look for information to confirm our opinions. Think contemporary American politics. Who do we interact with today? Those that agree with us. We watch and read news that *confirms* our views rather than *informs* our views. We engage and befriend people who verbally traffic within our perspective. We are firmly entrenched in Confirmation Bias.
- *The Attribution Bias*: The tendency to attribute other people's behavior to a flaw in their character or personality, while we attribute our own behavior to the situation. You know how this works: If some guy cuts you off in traffic, he is an idiot. But if you cut somebody off, it's because you are late to a very important commitment. If you have an underperforming employee, you conclude that he is unsalvageable. *"They just don't make people like they used to,"* you sigh. But if you have a stellar employee, then it's the result of your excellent leadership.

- *The Semmelweis Reflex*: The predisposition to deny new information that challenges your established views. Ignaz Semmelweis (1818-1865) was a Hungarian physician who observed that infants delivered by doctors at the Vienna General Hospital had a mortality rate three times higher than those delivered by midwives. He studied the deliveries and discovered the reason was that the midwives washed their hands between deliveries while the doctors did not. He published his findings in 1847.[3] Those doctors that started washing their hands saw a reduction in mortality rates to less than 1%. But many doctors were deeply offended by his suggestion that they were the actual cause of the higher mortality rate. After all, they were educated. They went into obstetrics to save lives, not to put them at risk.

  Keep in mind, these were pre-Lister and pre-Pasteur times. These were times when life was thought to be in the blood, and blood was perceived to be healthy. Many of the doctors of the day believed that a gentleman's hands would never carry disease.

<u>Collectivist Thinking</u>: Think pigeon-holing. This damages the soul of our culture and delegitimizes the individual. This follows tight on the heels of our Cognitive Biases and involves Lethargic Thinking. It is mentally assigning an individual to a group because of a position or view that he holds. It usually includes an element of moral condescension while placing everyone in a certain group that disagrees with me. Intellectual Collectivism is often displayed by titles, name-calling, and emotional conclusions. It causes us to see people as part of a group rather than as individuals with similarities.

To overcome these enemies of critical thinking, tomorrow's leader must have the courage to swim up the intellectual stream when necessary, and the confidence to play devil's advocate with peers, friends, and the majority.

Truthful or Honest Leader

Telling the truth is a behavior; honesty is a character trait. Theoretically, if we could teach our kids to be totally honest, we would never have to teach them to tell the truth.

We defined truth as "that which conforms to reality." Let's take a run at the definition of a lie. How about "the intent to deceive"? Toy with this for a moment. Is it possible for a person to tell the truth, and still lie?

One day a teacher was handed a homemade pie by one of her students. After dinner that night, she took a bite of the pie and it was terrible. She tried a second bite, but it was equally bad and it for sure wasn't going down the shoot. She took the pie and tossed it in the waste basket. The next morning the pie-maker approached the teacher and asked her, "How did you like my pie?"

She hemmed and hawed, and then hemmed and hawed again, and finally replied, "A pie of that quality sure doesn't last long around our household." A mildly amusing escape. The teacher was clever, but did she tell the truth? Sure. The pie didn't last long, and it was the direct result of the pie's quality. She told the truth. But did she lie? Careful here. Let me rephrase it. Did the teacher want the pie-maker to walk out with a picture of reality that was different from that which is? Yup! The teacher lied when she told the truth. Truth-telling is a behavior, but honesty is a character trait.

Can a person tell an untruth and still not lie? On November 3, 1948, the *Chicago Daily Tribune* ran the headline, **DEWEY DEFEATS TRUMAN**. It takes a long Google search to locate President Dewey. Did the *Tribune* tell the truth? Obviously not. But did they lie? Did they intend to deceive the public? Again, obviously not. They made other errors, including in judgment, but they sure weren't trying to trick the public into believing that Dewey had won the Presidency.

Did you ever have a boss who was a credit thief? Credit came down the line and he reached out through silence, by not giving credit where it was due—and stole some for himself. Truth-telling is a behavior, but honesty is a character trait.

Now, let's momentarily lay aside the more obvious moral implications of honesty and truth-telling and look at the utilitarian affect.

<u>Benefits of honesty</u>

1. *Believability*. Even when a liar tells the truth, he is not believed, but a person who is habitually honest is easily believed.
2. *Comfort with reality*. A painful truth can be more comforting than the long-term pain of deception.
3. *Predictability*. Remember that totally honest boss? You can just about predict what he will do in any given situation.
4. *Order*. It was Walter Scott who put it poetically: "Oh, what a tangled web we weave...when first we practice to deceive."[4] Some of us work, and live, in the tangled web of chaos. Wherever you find your sphere of influence, commit to the advancement of order through truth-telling.

5. *Less stress.* If you commit to honesty, then many of your daily decisions are already made before you show up for work. For the dishonest person, it is not so. They make numerous decisions daily, based on how it benefits them and their interests, rather than how it relates to reality. This causes increased stress.

When you have a budget, you are spending the money before it arrives. When you have a schedule, you are spending your time before it arrives. When you have honesty, you are making decisions before they arrive. Stress declines.

Here is your leadership challenge—develop a strong relationship with truth in your speech. Self-observe the precision of what you say in common conversation and self-correct when you exaggerate or distort.

Summary—Here are the building blocks and best practices that will prepare you for tomorrow's leadership challenges.

- Live and think in truth. Become comfortable with reality, even if it makes you uncomfortable.
- Be precise with your speech. Remember, even when a liar tells the truth they are not believed.
- Carefully weigh feedback from friends who give you a bargain-store mirror reflection.
- Make a habit of starting your analysis with the question, *to what end?*
- Look for a problem that you can practice the *Five Levels of Why* with.
- Ask yourself which of the four biases you are most influenced by and develop a strategy to minimize its influence.
- Listen to opposing views with the intent of learning rather than converting.
- Monitor your speech and listen for evidence of intellectual collectivism like name calling, group think, categorizing, excessive emotionalism, etc.

CHAPTER 9

A Meds-Free Stress Control

Assuming noble intent.

> Be kind,
> for everyone you meet is fighting a hard battle.
> —Anonymous

t's getting crazier out there, and life is tough to begin with. We are facing a serious storm and tomorrow's leaders must navigate through it.

For many of us, stress has become a dominant force in our lives. It can taint our perspective, distort our decisions, destroy our health, corrode our relationships, and numb the flavor of our life.

Now, stress is a big and complex subject. This chapter is a delicate attempt to avoid technical overinformation, while still laying enough groundwork for you to forge practical decisions that will give you some sense of control over the power of stress in your life.

First, I am not suggesting in the title that there is no need for anxiety-related medications. I, no doubt like you, have loved ones who have found these medications quite helpful when facing challenging circumstances. But I am saying that many people have found an effective option available for dealing with stress, and that is what we will be exploring.

Second, this chapter starts darkly but ends brightly, so stay with me. It isn't fair to you to suggest that the world we are walking into tomorrow will be increasingly sunshine and roses. In some respects, it is getting darker. The old hand-holding, "Kumbaya" approach to adversity is wearing thin and it isn't fair to you, or to those you lead, to suggest otherwise. So, let's hit this head on.

We are having difficulty coping with stress and it's taking a toll. It's taking a toll on our economy. According to the American Psychological Association, stress cost employers $300 billion in 2014.[1] It's taking a toll on our physical health. In 2017, 77% of Americans regularly experienced *physical* symptoms caused by stress. It's taking a toll on our *psychological* health. Again in 2017, 73% of Americans regularly experienced psychological symptoms caused by stress.[2] And it's not getting better. 48% feel their stress has increased over the past 5 years.[3]

Unfortunately, some are making poor final decisions or are checking out. Suicide is now the second leading cause of death for children, adolescents, and young adults ages 5 to 24,[4] and the general suicide rate has increased an average of 2% per year from 2006 to 2017.[5] We are going the wrong direction, and fast.

You get the point.

Stress—So What Is It?

Stress can be helpful. What is often referred to as positive stress is called *eustress*. Examples of eustress—or good stress—are a passionate kiss, getting married, buying a home, having a baby, or getting a promotion. Negative stress on the other hand, can be quite debilitating. This negative stress is sometimes called *distress*. Seeing that we have little difficulty dealing with positive stress, we are going to focus on the negative stress.

So, if we call the bad stress *negative stress*, then it must be our foe. Therefore, we need to get rid of it. Not so fast. Yes, there are good stress-relieving techniques, but techniques are in the domain of the *how-tos.*

Get out your telescope and let's zoom out for a moment. Is physical pain your friend or foe? Ask Ashlyn Blocker from Patterson, GA, who was born with a rare genetic condition called Congenital Insensitivity to Pain (CIP).[6] Researchers found that genetic mutations in both copies of the PRDM12 gene that she inherited from her mother and father—who are unaffected carriers of the defective gene—result in all the pain sensors of the body being turned off from birth. Ashlyn can feel pressure, and to a limited extent temperature, but she literally feels no pain and never has. At first blush, you might think that life would be amazing if lived pain free. Ashlyn and her parents would not share that view. Toddlers born with CIP can unintentionally injure themselves by chewing their tongues, cheeks, or fingers. In fact, Ashlyn can—and has—put her hand in boiling water without feeling any painful sensation.

I had a wonderful college professor who had an eccentric view of handling headaches. It was his decision to *never* take pain medication when a headache struck. (Not necessarily recommended!) His reasoning was that the headache was only a symptom of something else, like too much pizza or beer the night before, or not enough sleep, or possibly a brain tumor. If he took the pain medication, he went on to reason, he could be numbing the warning that a destructive behavior or disease was damaging his body. Physical pain is generally our annoying friend. It's telling us that what is happening to our body isn't good for us.

Here is how I see it. In some respects, pain is to your physical being what guilt is to your spiritual being and what stress is to your emotional being. All of them are frustrating friends telling us that if we continue as we are, then more bad stuff is going to happen.

Three Stress Arenas

The song is called "Stressed Out" by Twenty One Pilots, and the album it's on, *Blurryface*, has now gone platinum—seven times.[27] Here is where it gets interesting. Every album's sales drop off precipitously once the album ceases to be promoted. *Blurryface* has been no exception. However, streaming sites have picked up "Stressed Out," and it now continues to grow in popularity. In fact, the "Stressed Out" video has now been viewed over 1.2 *billion* times. Why? The lyrical profundity of Emily Dickinson is not at risk of being outshone by Twenty One Pilots. Why then has this midtempo rap-rock song grown in popularity instead of declined? Answer: It resonates with Americans today. Let's take a closer look at some of the lyrics to see why.

There are three areas of our lives that seem to provide the greatest amount of stress: people, time, and possession. If you cooked a meal and used these three ingredients, that dish would be called *work*. Work is where all three components come together. Let's take them one at a time.

Time: It's a value indicator. If I showed you my calendar, you could tell me what my core values are. Not what I think they are, not what I wish they were, but what they are. Time is a more reliable indicator of core values than money, because money comes and goes, but time only goes. And because time reflects our core values, much of our stress emanates from this area. The American Psychological Association sur-vey revealed that 60% of Americans indicated that work-related stress was "very" or "somewhat significant" in their life.[8]

The song "Stressed Out" expresses a longing for a different perspective on time this way:

Wish we could turn back time, to the good old days
When our momma sang us to sleep but now we're stressed out...
I'd make a candle out of it if I ever found it
Try to sell it, never sell out of it, I'd probably only sell one
It'd be to my brother, 'cause we have the same nose
Same clothes homegrown a stone's throw from a creek we used to roam...
We'll talk more about time in chapter 19.

<u>Possessions</u>: According to Market Watch, the number-one reason that Americans are stressed out is money.[9] Let's look at those lyrics again:

But it would remind us of when nothing really mattered
Out of student loans and tree-house homes we all would take the latter...
Used to dream of outer space but now they're laughing at our face
Saying, "Wake up, you need to make money..."

<u>People</u>: Each of us think that the only entirely normal person is *me* (and sometimes we have our suspicions about that). If you have two or more people, then you have conflict, and therefore stress. In fact, if you have *one* or more people, you have conflict, and therefore stress. "What was I thinking? Why did I say that?" Twenty One Pilots sing about this angst we all feel:

I was told when I get older all my fears would shrink
But now I'm insecure and I care what people think
My name's Blurryface and I care what you think
My name's Blurryface and I care what you think

Consider these stats: 48% of Americans said stress has a negative impact on their per-sonal and professional life. 54% said stress has *caused* them to fight with people close to them, and 26% report being alienated from a friend or family member *because* of stress.[10] Home is often where the best memories in life occur, but also the worst.

My Brain—So That Is How It Works

So, what can we do about it? I mean really—what *can* we do? Put your telescope away and dust off your microscope. Let's zoom in.

Several years ago, I was asked to write and present a five-day leadership workshop at the Pentagon. I took a risk and included the following information that zoomed in on the components and workings of the brain, unsure if it would connect. It did. Since then I have given that same workshop at the Pentagon several times. I have also included this section in many other workshops as well. I can tell you that when I return to an organization a year or two later, *this* is what they remember. So, if you are thinking about skipping a section, choose another one. This is practical empowerment.

Let me start with an apology to neuroscientists. This will be an oversimplification of the workings of the brain, but I understand that it's sufficiently accurate to support the point. It's always a risk to teach at the edge of one's knowledge, for it puts one at risk of falling off. I can see the edge from here.

Your brain does not consist of one mass of gray matter; it consists of a variety of components. These components fall into two categories: voluntary and involuntary—just like your body. Some organs in your body are voluntary, like your lungs. You can tell your lungs to quit breathing by holding your breath and they will stop. In a short period of time, they will win—but for the moment, you are in control. Your body also has some involuntary organs, like your heart. You can tell your heart to quit beating and it will simply ignore you. Your heart will continue to beat all the time. It doesn't matter whether you're awake or asleep. It doesn't matter whether you care, or whether you're even aware of it; it just continues to beat.

The three components of the brain that we will zoom in on are interconnected with neural pathways. These pathways provide channels of communication between the following components.

<u>Hippocampus</u> (Filing Cabinet): Here is a good place to start. This doesn't refer to an educational facility for large mammals—sorry. It's an *involuntary* component that functions like the old filing cabinet.

Ever since you were first aware that you were aware, you began to involuntarily absorb the sights, sounds, smells, pressures, and temperatures of life around you. These experiences entered through your senses and were stored in your hippocampus. All our life experiences are sorted and stored like files within the hippocampus, which becomes your long-term memory storage unit. It gives context to your life.

Here is what it looks like. If I tossed out a proper name like *Mary*, some people may have a positive reaction while others may have a negative reaction. Why? Some may think, "Cool—that's my mother's name." Others may think "Uncool—that's the name of my ex." Remember when you and your spouse were trying to decide on the name of your child? Did the files in your hippocampi collide?

If I tossed out the name *New York*, there would be opposite reactions. Some would think, "Cool—I had my honeymoon there." Others would think, "Uncool—I spent the longest month of my life there one weekend." When we have an experience, we involuntarily and instantaneously flip through the relevant files in our hippocampus and form a perspective of that life experience. We draw conclusions.

Back in the 1980s, my friend Bob and I took one week each year and went bow-hunting for deer near Spooner, Wisconsin. We parked the $300 camper in a clover field and had a great time. The deer were fairly safe, but we had a riot. I looked forward to that time fifty-one weeks a year.

Now, this was before the hunting industry really took off. We took skunk scent and put it on our boots to mask our human scent. Thinking back, it probably wasn't a good hunting tactic, because deer are probably not that fond of skunks either. To this day, forty years later, when that skunk comes out of hibernation and sacrifices his life under a tire on the road of progress, I have a totally different response from that of a normal person. Amazing memories of Bob and the woods of Wisconsin flood through my memory. Why? Because the files in my hippocampus are filled with entirely different experiences from those of other people. Now, I don't go out and buy skunk cologne, but I do have a totally different response. Your hippocampus constructs the context of your life, which provides the groundwork to interpret that life.

<u>Neocortex</u> (Computer): Generally, when people think of the brain, this is what they think of: the neocortex. It's the part of the brain that we use to consider, calculate, compare, contrast, and analyze. This component is located primarily behind your forehead and it's *voluntary*. It's like a computer. We can choose to think or not to think. We can choose to think quickly or slowly. We can choose to think deep or shallow thoughts. We can choose to think briefly or for extended periods of time. This is the part of the brain that really gets underused.

<u>Amygdala</u> (Smoke Detector): The amygdala is in the dead center of your brain. It's the size of an almond and it's *involuntary*. It, like radar, is constantly scanning the horizons of our life, looking for lions and tigers and bears. It's like a smoke detector looking for bad stuff. Once it perceives that a threat is near, it sends signals that release a flood of hormones, including cortisol and adrenaline, which ready you for action. The

old flight-or-fight response. Your heart begins to pound faster, your blood pressure increases, your muscles tighten, your breathing quickens, and your vision may narrow. This can work for us, or against us.

Suppose you had one of those days when everything turned sour. On top of that, your colleague, who has become a burr under your saddle, is in your face. You can feel in your body your amygdala beginning to engage. It begins to flash. Your jaw tightens, your breathing shallows and shortens, and the thought of his nose being introduced to your fist enters your mind. You can physically feel your anger growing.

Now, the amygdala is designed to continue flashing up to ninety seconds after the threat has subsided. Remember when your grandma told you to count to ten? She was eighty off.

Let's put this together. Your brain's components talk with each other through the neurocircuitry. Think of a neural pathway as a water hose. When the amygdala is fully flashing and you're mad and/or fearful, the neural pathway to the neocortex physically decreases in diameter. In fact, it can temporarily disengage. In a time of severe anger or fear, the amygdala can take over your brain and the neural pathway to the neocortex falls silent. If right now, as you're reading this book, a large explosion takes place right outside of your door, your amygdala will take over. Your physical response will engage, and you'll instantly forget about this book. Your amygdala will override your neocortex. Remember what the neocortex does? It thinks, considers, calculates, compares, and analyzes.

We don't do our best thinking when our amygdala is flashing. If you pull the file labeled *Stupid Things I Have Said and Done* out of your hippocampus, you would no doubt find that many of the things in that fat file occurred when your amygdala was flashing.

Can you stay angry longer than ninety seconds? Sure we can. Here is how it works. You are lying in bed at night after a frustrating day. Your "burr-under-the-saddle" idiot caught you off guard and was in your face. He was shouting crude, albeit false, accusations at you in front of your peers…and boss. You are now lying awake and thinking something like this: "The next time that happens, I am going to tell that village-robber…" You begin to rehearse the details of how you're going to tell him off and what precisely you're going to do to him. As you're previewing this in your mind, your amygdala begins to flash. You can feel your heart pounding; your throat tightens and your breathing shallows. Now, think this through. There has been no additional external threat and yet your amygdala has activated. What you're doing is backflushing from your neocortex to your amygdala. You're using your neocortex to think through the threat that does not exist, and it starts to reactivate your amygdala.

Have you ever met someone who lives a bitter life? This is what's going on inside them. They use their neocortex to backflush thoughts of revenge, which keeps their amygdala flashing. Think high levels of sustained stress. You don't need me to tell you what happens to a person who lives under high levels of sustained stress. There is a variety of creative ways in which they can lose their health.

Let's take this rubber to the road. Here is the big question that empowers us to move toward the light: Do you think it's possible for a person to control their amygdala when under a severe threat? As a Certified Flight Instrument Instructor, I have the opportunity to shepherd a private pilot to the next level, which is usually the Instrument Rating. Flying on instruments is an entirely different experience. I explain in the first preflight lesson that it can be possible for them to fly inverted and not be aware of it. At this point, many pilots—like myself when I was there—think something like, "I have lived with myself a long time and I think I know when I am upside down." So, we are up in the air flying some basic maneuvers under the hood. The hood is like a baseball cap on steroids. It has an extended and curled bill that prevents the pilot from seeing outside of the aircraft. The only visual access is the instrument panel. Most pilots-in-training have a fear in the back of their minds concerning an untimely contact with the terrain. Being under the hood exacerbates that fear. Sometimes, while executing a maneuver, the pilot might cross-control the aircraft and enter what the FAA refers to as an "unusual attitude." They may be upside down. Recovering an aircraft when under the hood can be a disconcerting experience, and their amygdala begins to flash. They try to bring the plane to wings level and sometimes they fail. They then ask for my assistance, using words like "Help! Help!" If we have enough altitude and airspeed, I don't help—for two reasons: one, the sheer enjoyment of the moment; and two, "Help! Help!" is not a good strategy during crises. The day is coming when they will have someone sitting in the right seat whom they love, and amygdala thinking can doom them.

The solution is to show and teach the pilot how to correct the aircraft and have them memorize the relevant checklist. This literally begins to re-hardwire their brain's neurocircuitry. You see, every time you choose your action when under duress, the neural pathway to the neocortex gets a little larger, which means it gets a little easier to think in times of crisis. It's just like when you go to the gym and you work your biceps with the curls. Each time you do a rep of ten, your biceps get a little bigger and it gets a little easier. Each time, in a moment of fear or anger, you make a choice to engage your neocortex instead of defaulting to your amygdala, the neural pathway to your neocortex gets bigger and bigger, which means it gets a little easier each time. This results in less stress.

If the US had an amygdala today, it would be fully flashing. Many people are irritable, fatigued, and listless. Tomorrow's leaders must understand how to get neocortex-engagement rather than amygdala-reaction from others. Once you understand this, opportunities abound for you to lower the stress level of those in your sphere of influence.

Here is one example. As leaders, our words can stimulate stress, or they can minimize it. Suppose you have an employee, or a kid, who has just messed up big time. You are frustrated and determined to get to the bottom of it. Here are a couple of options on how you can lead your inquiry. You can either ask, "Why did you do that?" or you can ask, "What was done here?"

How do you feel when you are on the receiving end of the question, "Why did you do that?" Don't you feel defensive, like you're under attack? This question activates the amygdala. That is not the part of the brain that we want people using. However, when you're asked, "What was done here?" there is an entirely different reaction. This question goes to the neocortex, not the amygdala. Here is how to remember. The word *why* goes to *motivation*, but the word *what* goes to *information*. Just using the different questions may activate different parts of the brain.

Plan—So Where to from Here?

Be honest now. What is your first reaction when you find an item missing from your desk? Isn't it, *who stole it?* What is your first reaction when you find conflicting stories from colleagues? Isn't it, *who lied?* Let's face it, our intellectual hard drive is bent toward the negative. If you want to inflict measurable damage on your personal stress load—start by giving others the benefit of the doubt. Better yet, assume the best in them. Discipline yourself to start every conversation by **assuming noble intent**.

So, what does that look like? I have been told that I'm a Type-A driver. It used to be that if a jerk pulled out in front of me, I would give him a piece of my mind (a piece that, candidly speaking, I couldn't afford to donate). Here is how I solved it. (I have many flaws but this one I have gotten a handle on.) Now when I get cut off in traffic, I *assume noble intent.* I ask myself: "Did they just find out their eight-year-old daughter has cancer? Did he just receive a bank notification that he will be losing his home? Did she just get served divorce papers?" It works! My traffic stress has collapsed, and it is amazing.

Here is your leadership challenge—develop the stress-reducing habit of starting each conversation, and each relationship, by **assuming noble intent**. If their intent is otherwise, then you can quickly adapt. To a large extent, character is nothing more than habits long endured.

Summary—Here are the building blocks and best practices that will prepare you for tomorrow's leadership challenges.

- Identify three work related stressors and premeditate how you will respond with your neocortex rather than defaulting to your amygdala.
- Identify a deep-seated joy, gratitude, relationship, blessing, or goal that you can marinate in when bitterness tries to hack into your neocortex and paralyze you through repetition by default.
- Consciously begin each conversation in the next three days with the assumption of noble intent.

CHAPTER 10

Subconsciously Motivating Others

Embracing intrinsic value.

Every job from the heart is,
ultimately, of equal value.
The nurse injects the syringe;
the writer slides the pen;
the farmer plows the dirt;
the comedian draws the laughter.
Monetary income is the perfect deceiver of a man's true worth.
—CRISS JAMI

t was troubling. The Federal Employee Viewpoint Survey (FEVS), issued annually to US federal employees, revealed a troubling trend—so much so that it caught the eye and interest of the Obama administration. Particularly, three areas surfaced across the federal spectrum that were, and are, not dissimilar to those expressed by their cousins in the private sector.

The three areas of concern were:

- Satisfaction with leadership
- Satisfaction with supervisory support
- Intrinsic work experience

During the latter years of the Obama administration, the US Office of Personnel Management (OPM) was tasked with confronting these concerns. OPM invested serious time and resources in designing a training course titled *Maximizing Employee Engagement*. I was tasked with the responsibility of teaching the original training course, as well as training the trainers.

A central theme of the course is the same question that tomorrow's leader must face: How do you effectively motivate a person in a materialistic—and some would argue, narcissistic—age, one in which there is a growing sense of entitlement?

Before we can address this question, we have an obligation to address a school of thought that counters the premise of this question. Some would argue that a leader cannot essentially motivate another person. They retreat to the dusty phrase, "You can lead a horse to water, but you can't make him drink." I share this countering view, but only to a point. It is true, of course, that every person has free will and therefore is ultimately responsible for the decisions they make, the words they choose, and the behaviors they display. But I part paths with this countering view, and its equestrian motto, at this point. It is true that *you can lead a horse to water, but you can't make him drink*. But it is equally true that you can feed him salt, and salt stimulates thirst. That is what high-impact motivational leaders see, and that is essentially where they focus.

Let's start with a dead end. There are some increasingly clever ideas for incentivizing employees, several of which I use and recommend. (If you're looking for a crisp and inexpensive resource, *1501 Ways to Reward Employees* by Bob Nelson is a good place to start.[31]) As clever and practical as some of these extrinsic ideas are, however, they ultimately fail to fully address the question of how to motivate a person in such a way that it fundamentally changes him or her.

To do so, we need to understand the two avenues of motivation—extrinsic and intrinsic—as well as *how to*, and *when to* use each. Whether you're a supervisor of employees, a coach of players, a teacher of students, a health-care provider of patients, or a parent of kids, this section should help you.

Motivating—Extrinsic or Intrinsic?

Motivation is generally divided into two categories: extrinsic and intrinsic. Extrinsic motivators focus on the carrot-and-the-stick approach. "If you do this, then you get that benefit, or you avoid getting that consequence." Intrinsic motivators focus on connecting a person to that which is internally meaningful. It is the tethering to significance when it comes to motivation. A leader will struggle with building these tethers if they're lacking a firm personal conviction that every person has intrinsic value. If that child doesn't think she has intrinsic value, she can't fool me—I still believe it. If that employee doesn't behave like he has intrinsic value, he can't fool me—I still believe it. Maturity is the ability to handle immaturity in others. It appears to me that when this conviction is absent, the leader tends to place their motivational hope disproportionately on extrinsic motivators and ends up reacting to reactions.

PEER-LEADER QUOTE

Leadership is constantly asking oneself the question,
"Would I follow me?"

WILDER SMITH
Branch Manager
TSA Intelligence Planning & Programs Division

To get a working grasp on this, let's explore six Motivational Comparisons. Check out Exhibit 10. 1. and then let's explore it together.

Exhibit 10. 1.

MOTIVATIONAL COMPARISONS

	EXTRINSIC (Carrot/stick – If you do this, then you get that.)	**INTRINSIC** (Tethering to Significance)
Durations	Short-term	Long-term
Applications	Mechanical Skills	Rudimentary Cognitive skills and above
Tethers	Happiness	Purpose
Sources	Laws	Values
Relationship with work	Compliance	Engagement
Authority	Manager	Leader

1. *Tether*: Extrinsic motivators tether people to happiness, while intrinsic motivators tether people to meaning or purpose. *And the downside to happiness is what?* you may ask. Nothing in and of itself, unless it stands alone.

    Extrinsic: How do you think your employees would answer the question, *What do you think is the greatest motivator for people at work?* They may give you an answer that I frequently hear: Money. But is money the greatest motivator? The answer is a firm *maybe*. It depends. If your kids can't eat tomorrow unless you bring home a check today, then money is the main motivator. And should be in that case.

    Intrinsic: Here is how we're put together. We're made to achieve.

    OK, parents, hang on. Happiness comes from receiving, but meaning comes from giving. When our kids have responsibilities and they learn to accept and own those responsibilities, they develop tethers to significance. Those tethers may look like discipline, overcoming adversity, rebounding from failure, and persisting through opposition.

    Start small and work big. If you turn it on, you turn it off. If you drop it, you pick it up. If you break it, you fix it. If you open it, you close it. If you borrow it, you return it. You work on developing a sense of ownership for their sphere of influence.

    First, be *responsible* for your sphere of influence. Second, *improve* your sphere of influence. Make it better than when you found it. Make people better than when you found them. It's a little unrealistic to think that we're going to make the world better if we can't even make our own bed. Start by taking care of the little things.

    "Watch the pennies and the dollars will take care of themselves" is a wise saying (falsely attributed to Ben Franklin, but most likely coined by William Lowndes).

    Same principle. Changing the world starts by being responsible for our little sphere of influence (pennies).

    A caution for parents: Because we don't want to see our kids struggle, we intercept their challenges and end up teaching them weakness. We bubble-wrap their lives to prevent risk and end up teaching fear. We don't want them to taste failure, so we intervene and end up teaching them to be quitters. Much of motivational meaningfulness is the result of a struggle for an outcome (like a butterfly exiting a cocoon). In each of these cases of parental interference, the result in the child is immediate happiness; or at least less suffering, but with the potential loss of longer-term meaning.

2. <u>Authority</u>: Extrinsic motivators are frequently found in the toolbox of the manager and intrinsic motivators are more frequently found in the toolbox of the leader.

3. <u>Application</u>: Extrinsic motivators are most effective when used with mechanical or repetitive skills while intrinsic motivators are most effective when used with tasks involving rudimentary cognitive skills and above.

4. <u>Work Relationship</u>: Extrinsic motivators are great tools when we need employees to comply. Extrinsic motivators are often effective in compliance scenarios that require adherence to safety and legal requirements. Intrinsic motivators are great when we need employees to voluntarily engage. Anytime a person voluntarily invests their time and possessions in anything, their affections follow their investment.

5. <u>Source</u>: Extrinsic motivators originate outside of the person being motivated. These extrinsic motivators can take the form of policies, rules, or regulations. Intrinsic motivators internally tap into their values and priorities.

6. <u>Duration</u>: Extrinsic motivators tend to be short lived while intrinsic motivators tend to have longer shelf lives. Did you ever have the possibility of a job or a promotion which would provide a nice increase in income? You thought that if you could just get that new job, or that promotion, then you would be the most motivated employee ever. And you got it, and you were. You were so happy, and you were the most motivated worker ever. For two weeks. Happiness does not have the sustaining power that meaning, or purpose, has.

In fact, happiness is analogous to a trait found in some medications. Some medications lose their potency, requiring greater doses to retain the original effect. This is how we can trap ourselves into an addiction. You may think it cool that your boss surprises you the first year with a Thanksgiving turkey. The second year you begin to expect it. If on the third year you don't get the turkey, then you may feel robbed.

The span between gratitude and expectation is getting shorter in our culture today and the shelf life of happiness is getting even shorter. Meaning, on the other hand, is like wine. It improves over time.

Summary—Here are the building blocks and best practices that will prepare you for tomorrow's leadership challenges.

- Check your reactions to reactions and modify if needed. Remember, maturity is the ability to handle immaturity in others.
- Search your motivational tactics to ascertain whether you are overdependent on extrinsic motivators.
- Develop a toolbox of extrinsic motivators for mechanical and repetitious tasks, and a separate toolbox of intrinsic motivators for responsibilities that involve at least rudimentary cognitive skills.

CHAPTER 11

Stress-Free Delegation, or at Least Minimized

Strategy for tackling the number-one reason supervisors fail.

When you delegate tasks, you create followers.
When you delegate authority, you create leaders.
—CRAIG GROESCHEL

f you have ever supervised anyone, then you'll know what I'm about to describe. You delegate responsibilities with seeming clarity, but a few employees keep returning with questions. They show you their work and they seem insecure. They seek confirmation from you that they are correctly meeting your expectations. They often look to you to solve the smallest of problems. If you fail to decisively address this, then they can quickly become comfortable in being your personal time thieves.

You are not alone. In many respects, improper delegation has become the number-one reason that supervisors fail. What to do?

Here are the solid components that make up effective delegation.

1. *Revitalize your paradigm*: Reevaluate your supervisory paradigm. Remember the scenario I mentioned earlier?

   ... in the work environment, senior management looks at an employee who manages their work well. They utilize resources well, they solve their own problems, and they achieve a desired outcome. So, senior management promotes them. The assumption is, if a person can manage their work well, then they should be able to manage the worker well.

Not so. You were promoted because you managed your work well. You are apparently a good problem solver. If you find yourself reactively solving their problems, then you need to dust off your supervisory paradigm. Essentially, you're not getting paid to solve *their* problems. You're getting paid to teach them to solve their problems. When you instinctively take ownership for their problems, then you're teaching them to depend on you. It may be personally rewarding, but you will end up spending more time putting out their fires than doing your own work. Worse yet, your employees may underdevelop. Spoon-fed employees grow more slowly.

How do you revitalize and retain your supervisory paradigm? Form your perspective and prepare your development question.

- **Perspective**: *Good leaders are remembered for how many followers they create, but great leaders are remembered for how many leaders they create.* This is a great coffee-cup quote, but the reality is, it requires raw courage.

  Think of parenting. Every parent aspires to see their kids surpass them. They want to see them develop. They want to see them become better people and more successful. So does the secure leader. Unfortunately, there are too many supervisors that hoard information because they are fearful that others around them may surpass them. Develop a deep-seated satisfaction in seeing those in your sphere of influence excel.

- **Practice**: Prepare yourself with a development question in lieu of your reactive solution. Have it ready to go when the moment arises. The question I recommend is "If you were me, what would you do?" Ask it early; ask it often. If you ask it consistently, they'll still keep coming to you for assistance, but they'll know the question they'll be facing. They'll start thinking from your perspective.

  This question will help you distinguish the employees with lower *competence* from those with lower *confidence*. Listen carefully to their answers and you will discover that they either have a competence issue, or a confidence issue, or possibly both. As a supervisor, you will address these in separate ways. However, if you instinctively jump in and solve their problems without asking your development question, then you're supervising both issues in the same way.

2. *Filter your responsibility*: Use the **4-D Time Management Filter** (See Exhibit 11. 1., Anonymous, 2018). Here is how this works. You have inherited a new project. You already have a full plate and you're a little uncertain how it will get done. Use this vetting filter to guide you to your best option.

Exhibit 11. 1.
4-D Time Management Filter

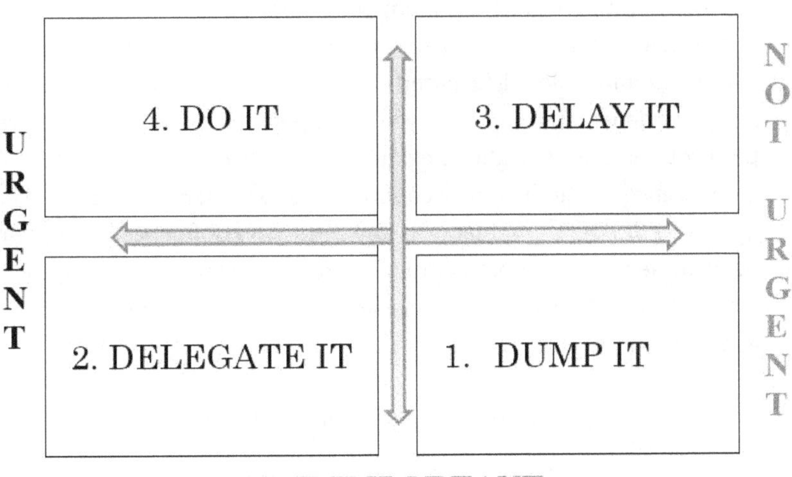

I. *Dump it.* First decision—decide *if* it needs to be done.

Let your supervisory paradigm take over. Be careful to avoid instinctively jumping in and completing the responsibility yourself. That should be your *last* consideration.

Instead, this is where you start, because this is your value filter. Ask yourself candid questions like, *If this is dumped, what ramifications will occur?* If the project survives this filter, then take it to step two.

II. *Delegate it.* Second decision—decide *who* will do it.

Your next consideration is to match the employee with the desired outcome. Consider the four following areas:

1. Relevant skills
2. Resistance level
3. Personal workload
4. Pivotal intangibles (effort, ethics, and people skills)

III. *Delay it.* Third decision—decide *when* to do it.

If no one else is capable or available, and you don't have the time, then you may need to delay it. Be sure to record your start and completion dates so it doesn't inadvertently get ushered by procrastination into the Dump filter.

IV. *Do it.* Final decision—do it.

I am sure you have this one covered.

3. *Choose your role*: You need to remember that delegation is also a great personnel-development tool, so select your employee carefully. Identify what your continuing role will be based upon your employee's level of competence and confidence. If your employee's competence and confidence are high, then you can use a straight delegation approach. However, if your employee's competence is high but their confidence is low, then adapt a more encouraging role. If their competence is low but their confidence is high, then you need to adapt to a more instructive role as a teacher. (See Exhibit 11. 2.) However, if both their competence and confidence are low, then you want to adapt to a more direct role.

Personnel Development Strategy

Exhibit 11. 2.

<table>
<tr><td rowspan="2">Skills/Abilities</td><td>High</td><td>ENCOURAGE</td><td>DELEGATE</td></tr>
<tr><td>Low</td><td>DIRECT</td><td>TEACH</td></tr>
<tr><td></td><td></td><td>Low</td><td>High</td></tr>
<tr><td></td><td></td><td colspan="2">Motivation/Confidence</td></tr>
</table>

4. *Clarify your boundaries*: Here is where delegation often breaks down. The employee is unsure of what your boundaries are. They may end up taking more latitude in the project than you had intended, rendering the outcome of the project far afield of what you had in mind. Or, they may go the opposite direction. They may feel unduly bound to strict instructions when you really wanted them to invest more personal discretion in their creativity and decision making. To avoid this confusion, use one of the following three words when you delegate.

    - Is my delegation a *suggestion*?: "Here is an idea or two that you might want to consider, but you make the final decision."
    - Is my delegation a *recommendation*?: "Here is how I think you should accomplish the project. If you see differently, please get back with me and we will decide together."
    - Is my delegation a *directive*?: "Here is how you will do it."

5. *Outcomes rather than tasks*: This is your strongest development tool. When possible, delegate the outcome of the project rather than just the tasks. When you only delegate tasks, your employee may feel like they are being manipulated. They may feel like you don't have confidence in them, and their trust level takes a hit. However, when you delegate the outcome, they feel a sense of ownership. They sense that you are investing trust in them and in their abilities. They will be more likely to solve problems on their own, locate needed resources, and complete the project on time and on budget. Remember the tethering principle—people buy into vision more than they buy into plans. This teaches your employee to begin with the end in mind. You are making leaders, not semi-programmable robots.

PEER-LEADER QUOTE

Tomorrow's leader is one who delivers outcomes at the speed of life, business, technology and innovation.

ROB DENSON
President
Des Moines Area Community College

6. *Monitoring schedule*: Did you ever have a boss delegate a responsibility to you, and then in a couple of weeks unexpectedly call you into their office? What

was your reaction in that moment? Many employees would immediately begin to wonder if there was a problem, or if they had done something out of line. You remember in high school when the voice of the principle boomed your name through the intercom, followed by a directive to report to their office? It has that kind of a feel to it. Here is another place that trust can take a needless hit. To avoid this, communicate your monitoring schedule when you delegate the project. "In two weeks, we will sit down and review your progress and see if you need any assistance." If they know the monitoring points in advance, they sense that you are on their side.

7. *Provide resources*: One of the more frustrating aspects of delegation for the employee is the knowledge that they are being asked to do something, but the necessary resources were not provided to successfully complete the delegated responsibility.

8. *Identify the go/no-go*: You have been handed a high-value responsibility and you are now weighing the option of delegating it. But you are hesitant. You know that if you want the job done right, you have to do it yourself. This sentiment leads to time-debt, where you feel like you always owe people time from yesterday, and it takes a great personnel-development tool off the table. So, you're confronted with the question: "Do I really want to delegate it when I am unsure they will complete it correctly, and then I have to face my boss with failure? Or, do I do it myself and step into the time-debt trap?"

    There is a way that you might be able to delegate this high-value responsibility and still sleep peacefully at night. Establish a go/no-go point. Set up an early monitoring point. If you discover at that point that your employee is mortally failing, you still have time to step in and salvage the project. However, before that monitoring point is reached, your employee still enjoys your trust in them and in their abilities.

9. *Follow up*: The responsibility of tomorrow's leader doesn't end with the successful completion of the delegated responsibility. Here is a great opportunity to invest in your employee by teaching through a project review, and by authentically commending him or her. This should be your final monitoring point, and it is ripe with great opportunity to invest value in your employee. Seize it.

Summary—Here are the building blocks and best practices that will prepare you for tomorrow's leadership challenges.

- Conduct a self-assessment of your delegation skills to ascertain whether you are over-doing and under-delegating.
- Try the 4-D Time Management Filter (see Exhibit 11. 1.) to schedule your task assignments.
- Place the initials of your team members in the four squares of the Personnel Development Tool (see Exhibit 11. 2.) based on their competence and confidence levels. Modify your role in delegating based on your assessments.

CHAPTER 12

Communicating Is Not Dueling Soliloquies

Secrets to ratcheting up your verbal credibility.

Wise men speak because they have something to say;
Fools because they have to say something.
—Plato

ere's one reason not to skip this chapter—your career advancement. Your career advancement, regardless of your vocational choice, will depend in large part on how well you perform in two areas: technical skills and relationships. Let's consider technical skills first. It doesn't matter whether you're a white-collar or blue-collar worker, your impact will increase as your communication skills increase. It's difficult to picture a job where improved communication would not also improve job efficiency and effectiveness. I have observed brilliant individuals whose careers were stymied because they had difficulty with public presentations. I have observed impaired assembly lines because of vague instructions. Communication breakdowns are still one of the most common job-related complaints in the workforce today.

Secondly, communication skills are the grease of human relationships. It was Helen Keller who keenly observed, "When you lose your vision, you lose contact with things. When you lose your hearing, you lose contact with people." Improved communication will increase relationships with people.

Improving your communication skills will contribute to improved job effectiveness and relationship building—the cornerstones of career advancement.

Communication Breakdowns

There are five primary ways that communication breaks down in the workplace today.

1. <u>Absent communication</u>: "Why didn't I get the memo? Why wasn't I informed? Where did you get that information?"
2. <u>Partial communication</u>: The email informed you of the nature, time, duration, and location of the meeting, but not the date.
3. <u>Ambiguous communication</u>: Your colleague asks you, following the meeting, "What exactly are we supposed to be doing now?"
4. <u>Tardy communication</u>: You get an email notifying you that today's 2:00 p.m. meeting will be postponed until tomorrow. The email was sent at 2:15 p.m.
5. <u>Overcommunication</u>: Everyone has experienced sitting in a meeting where a verbal narcissist, who has fallen in love with the sound of his own voice, drones on and on. You look around the room, and it's apparent by the looks in your colleagues' eyes that their porch lights are on, but no one is home. Or, you listen to someone make their point—repeatedly. They haven't learned the need to stop drilling once they strike oil.

Or, you receive tome-like emails that are heavy with too much information. The result? The email isn't read.

Of the five miscommunications, *overcommunication* has become the most pervasive. Our culture has decreasing patience for anything that requires extended focus. Sadly, there are those that think that the future of baseball may be at risk. It's the only major sport without a clock, and it takes too much time. In this Twitter- and texting-driven world, people aren't willing to read long emails, books, or articles.

Your solution to avoid the seduction of overcommunication is verbal economy. When speaking, strive to say as much as possible in the shortest period. When writing, work at using the minimum number of words to accomplish your literary mission. Designing brief but effective communiqués takes time and skill. Pascal told us in 1657,[1] "The present letter is a very long one, simply because I had no leisure to make it shorter."[32]

Do you remember that great two-hour-long speech delivered at Gettysburg National Cemetery on November 18, 1863, by Edward Everett? Neither do I. However, you may remember the three-minute speech that followed, *The Gettysburg Address*, by President Abraham Lincoln. Brevity is invigorating and memorable.

Writing Emails

Here are a few brief considerations that tomorrow's leader needs to consider when writing:

False bravery: Social media has unleashed a sense of false courage in writers. People are writing things they would never say to someone on the phone, let alone face to face. You may want to consider using a different communication avenue when communicating with an unhappy reader about sensitive or distressing information. Speaking, as opposed to writing, may help the listener stay focused; this is preferable to the writing of hostile things under the false guise of bravery.

Lists: Lean on lists. Think about how readers consume online news: "Seven ideas for..."; "Ten suggestions to..."; "Three secrets of...." Paragraphs may contain all the information you want included in your email, but lists make it easier for the reader to track. I prefer numbered lists over bullets, because it becomes a natural to-do list, and you can refer to a specific item by number, rather than by description.

Subject lines: If you are communicating a single point or question, put it in your subject line. If your email is longer, then consider using the subject line as a tease for something you will address in the body of your email.

Active voice: Many of us overuse the passive voice when writing, especially those in the federal sector. The active voice can incite attention, while the passive voice feels dry and objective. "You are so loved by me," simply doesn't incite the warm feelings that "I love you so much" does.

"Good writing is supposed to evoke sensation in the reader—not the fact that it's raining but the feeling of being rained upon"[2] (E. L. Doctorow).[33]

Presenting in Public

If you are serious about developing your leadership skills for tomorrow, then the skill of public speaking should rise toward the top of your list.

Many of us struggle, in varying degrees, with *glossophobia*—the fear of speaking in public. It has derailed many aspiring leaders, while overcoming it has provided vertical access to many less competent leaders. Start developing your public presentation skills with the following:

Speak to an individual: You have now been introduced and have arrived at the podium. Instantly, you feel all those eyes on you, and your own voice sounds like a stranger. Fear settles in. Try this: Carefully select a few seemingly attentive individuals sitting in different sections of the audience. Zone out the rest of the group. Establish eye contact with each one, and occasionally move your eye contact from one to the other. This not only helps minimize your fear, but it also helps you subconsciously become more personal with your language. For instance, you might find yourself saying "you," instead of "all of you."

Prepare, prepare, prepare: Even the most experienced speaker encounters fear when giving a presentation that contains the totality of their knowledge on the subject. Avoid the fear of falling off the edge of your knowledge: prepare, prepare, prepare.

Understand your objective: Public speakers are often known by their focus.

- Focused on self: Both rookie and veteran speakers can find their focus here. For rookies—because they feel the eyes of the audience on them and they hear their own voice—their focus is on themselves. It makes it more difficult to both present the material and connect with the audience. Veteran speakers may also focus on themselves, but for different reasons. The words of a veteran speaker may drip with self-regard and self-interest. They are promoting themselves. The effect of the veteran's focus shares that of the rookie's focus: a diminished impact from the material and a disconnect from the audience.

- Focused on material: You remember that teacher in school who loved their subject? For me, it was a math teacher. He didn't struggle with self-focus. He loved math—so much so that he got lost in his material, to the extent that he became oblivious and the students became disengaged (except for a few math whizzes). When you speak in public, you're not teaching material; you're teaching people.

- Focused on audience: This is where you want to end up. You know your material so well that your passion shifts to the audience. A small percentage of public speakers regularly resides here. Become one of them.

Take a video selfie: Suppose you are scheduled to present a critical public presentation in the near future, and you want to be prepared. What to do? Experience is your best solution. But you don't have time, so experience won't help you now.

1. Try this uncomfortable crash course in lieu of experience. Kindly ask those who reside with you to depart, temporarily. This is best accomplished in solitude. Dust off your video recording device and take a video selfie of you giving your full presentation. Don't start and stop it. Just keep taping regardless of mistakes. Once completed, sit down and watch the full presentation from start to finish.

2. Back it up and review it a second time—only this time through, mute it. Evaluate your visual presentation skills. Be sure to take notes. Watch your body language. Do you tug at your shirt or skirt when you're nervous? Do you scratch your nose or glance up and to the right when you have a weak point? Do you subtly roll your eyes when you make a mistake? Because you've lived with yourself for quite a while, you may not be aware of some of your annoying visual tells.

3. Review it a third time. Evaluate your oral presentation. This time reverse it— kill the picture and listen to your words. Do you use a lot of filler words like *you know, kinda, like, so, actually,* and *literally*? Do you speak too fast or too slow? Do you speak too softly or too loudly? Do you have a strong opening and closing? Does your humor work? Is the presentation too long or too short? Does point two have anything to do with point three?

Listening—It's a Skill

St. Francis of Assisi told us at the beginning of the thirteenth century, "Grant that I may not so much seek…to be understood, as to understand…" Stephen Covey approached it like this: "Seek first to understand, then to be understood."[3]

If you study people who are great communicators, you will find great listeners. If you study people who are poor communicators, you often find poor listeners. Listening is difficult; and people are increasingly less patient when it comes to listening. This will put even more pressure on you, as tomorrow's leader, to up your game. It may be no coincidence that *listen,* and *silent* contain the same letters.

Start here—develop the conviction that everyone knows something that you don't know. When others speak, prepare yourself as though they have something of value that you don't have. Listen with both your ears...and eyes. Look them in the eye and listen for value

PEER-LEADER QUOTE

*Tomorrow's leader is one who considers differing views
and acts based on principles and integrity.*

DONALD G. KLEIN
Deputy to the President
National Credit Union Administration

Why is listening so difficult? There usually isn't one simple answer. Because we are complex beings, the answer is often complex and nuanced. Consider some of those nuanced reasons.

Why We Don't Hear Others (author unknown)

If you want to listen so you really hear what others say, make sure you're not a:

- **Mind reader.** You'll hear little or nothing as you think, "What is this person really thinking or feeling?"
- **Rehearser.** Your mental tryouts for "Here's what I'll say next" tune out the speaker.
- **Filterer.** Some call this selective listening—hearing only what you want to hear.
- **Dreamer.** Drifting off during a face-to-face conversation can lead to an embarrassing "What did you say?" or "Could you repeat that?"
- **Identifier.** If you connect everything you hear to your experience, you probably didn't really hear what was said.
- **Comparer.** When you get sidetracked assessing the messenger, you're sure to miss the message.
- **Derailer.** Changing the subject too quickly soon tells others you're not interested in anything they have to say.
- **Sparrer.** You hear what's said but quickly belittle or discount it. That puts you in the same class as the derailer.
- **Placater.** Agreeing with everything you hear just to be nice or to avoid conflict does not mean you're a good listener.

We have established that listening is even more essential for future leaders than it is for contemporary leaders. Now let's flip it in the opposite direction. How well do people listen to you? Do you know? Do you care? If you care, but don't know, here is a good evaluative tool for you.

Ten ways to determine people aren't listening to you when you talk:

1. *Your words are met with a Charles Manson-like stare.* Enough said!
2. *Your lines are stepped on.* People start talking before you finish.
3. *You rely on repetition to get things done.* Saying it once doesn't make it happen, so you find yourself repeating and repeating.
4. *You give a presentation and your audience is snoring.* Seems obvious.
5. *You face "sentence-disconnects."* You're talking about the need to move the project deadline and you hear, "How about those Cubs?"
6. *Your ideas become "plops."* You toss out what you believe to be a plausible solution in a brainstorming session, and it's met with silence from your colleagues. No one says, "Great idea," or "bad idea," or even the token "interesting idea," which often means "bad idea." It's just met with stony silence.
7. *You hear answers to questions you didn't ask.* We've all seen this done to others, and have had it done to us, so look for a pattern. That may tell you something.
8. *You see repeated subject changes.* This is first cousin to sentence-disconnects. You have trouble keeping people on track. They're chasing rabbits and you have trouble holding them on topic.
9. *You see frozen body language.* Unresponsive body language is often an indication that they have already checked out of your conversation.
10. *You depend on credibility cosigners like "I promise."* My dad tried to teach us as kids to be wary of those who depend on verbal cosigners. Here is how it works. If you lean repeatedly on phrases like, "I promise I will do it," or "I guarantee it will happen," you may be subconsciously indicating that you know your word is soft. If a person with credibility says, "I will do it," they don't feel the need to add a cosigner like, "I promise" to strengthen their word.

Establishing Your Verbal Credibility

Can you picture this person: when they speak, everyone listens? They have figured out how to construct trust with the way they speak. Think of the advantages they have.

Suppose you get an ambiguous email from a person who is a burr under your saddle, and you get the exact same email—verbatim—from a person with high verbal credibility. Human nature leads us to fill in the blanks that are left from the ambiguity. With the person who is the burr under our saddle, we tend to fill in the blanks with negative assumptions, but tend to make positive assumptions when filling in the blanks with the person who has verbal credibility.

One of the concepts I teach when coaching is *digital flash*. Everyone has one. You know how that window flashes onto your computer screen when you receive an email, or how you get that flash-notification that you have a voice mail? Your instant reaction to that digital flash may give you an indication of what you think of that person. For some people, we groan when we see their name in the digital flash; for others we just yawn; but for people who have earned verbal credibility, we are inclined to respond promptly. Develop your *digital flash* by increasing your verbal credibility, and you will find an improved response time.

How? How do you earn that verbal credibility? Here are ten ways to build verbal credibility.

1. *Be specific.* Imagine you are a juror and Witness #1 says that the burglary took place last week. Witness #2 says that it took place last Thursday. However, Witness #3 says that it occurred at 2:10 p.m. last Thursday while he was watching *Wheel of Fortune*, and that it took place during the first commercial. Which of the three would you be most inclined to believe? Especially when we get frustrated, we move away from specifics. Stay focused on the specific and avoid exaggerations and generalities.

2. *Avoid absolutes.* If you have ever been to marriage counseling, you probably have already heard this one. Avoid absolutes like "you always…" and "you never…." Never use absolutes; always avoid them!

3. *Avoid flattery.* Petty and insincere flattery comes across as manipulative. Spamming everyone with meaningless niceties does not strengthen your word.

4. *Stop phubbing.* Ready for a new word? It is a contraction of *phone-snubbing*. When someone is speaking to you, lose the device. Multitasking with conversations usually ends poorly. Focus on one at a time.

5. *Use the active voice.* The active voice helps build traction points.

6. *Avoid verbal cosigners.* Let the credibility of your word stand alone without the crutch of a cosigner like "I promise" or "I guarantee."

7. *Be honest.* Here is where it gets tough. (Please refer to the section titled *Truthful or Honest Leader* in chapter 8.)

8. *Become a verbal economist (not a verbal narcissist).*

9. *Avoid verbal overconfidence.* With the advent of social media, we have become a writing culture. The primary means of communication is shifting from oral to writing. One of the outcomes of this transition is an overconfidence in words, but a disinterest in delivery, resulting in what sounds like an oral email. Tomorrow's leader recognizes that the power of voice inflection, volume, pauses, cadence, body language, and eye contact are powerful communication tools to be leveraged.

10. *Believe your own words.* If you don't, they won't.

It is now 7:00 p.m. and your eight-year-old Johnny is playing his favorite video game. You inform him that at 7:30 p.m. the video game goes up and the homework comes out. At 7:45 p.m. you notice that he is still playing and that there is no homework in sight. Right here is where parents display whether they believe their own words or not. Would you agree that most, if not all, kids know where *the line* is? If the parent doesn't draw *the line* here, then they are informing the child that they don't even believe their own words. Some common substitutes are the numeric method ("on the count of three…"); or the decibel method, where the child knows he needs to listen when the volume reaches a certain point; or the birthname method, "Johnny Mark, I told you…."

Regardless of which method a parent chooses, they are disbelieving their own word and thereby teaching the child not to listen to them the *first time*. Before you speak or write, think through the consequences, or your next move, if your words receive no response. Typically, the more meeting reminders the boss sends to the team, the greater the indication that he/she doesn't believe his/her own word.

Communicating Tool for the Future

Storytelling! Seriously.

There is a time to persuade others using facts and data. Know your audience. But tomorrow's leader is discovering the power of persuading through dynamic storytelling.

Why is storytelling so powerful, and why is it the communication tool for tomorrow?

Let's step back and take a larger view. Join me at Google Maps. Let's zoom out until the entire world is in view. Now disconnect as a member of humanity and zoom back in; become a disinterested observer of the activities that are taking place on this round ball. You observe that it is teeming with all kinds of life forms. One of these life forms seems to be superior. They have opposable thumbs, superior intellect, complex communications, the capacity to think about thought, the ability to observe history past one generation, and the ability to develop complex strategies. You also note a very peculiar behavioral difference between this advanced species and all the others—a preoccupation with images.

You peek into their houses and you see images on the walls. Not just any images, but images of the inhabitants. You see images of landscapes that they could also observe by simply looking out of their windows. You go to Egypt and see the colored images from days of old that display their leaders, their women, their victories, and their gods. You look at their early days of living in caves and see stick images of animals, battles, and landscapes on their walls. No other species does this. No crane draws an image in the sand of an island from an aerial viewpoint. No wolf draws a charcoal picture of that deer from last fall's feast.

This superior species even builds structures that do nothing more than house images. No one lives there; only images on the walls. Get this: they *pay money* to go inside and view these images. Images of people, some of whom they have seen. Images of landscapes, some of which they have visited. Not only do they pay to *see* images, but they pay handsomely to *own* some of them. They will pay millions of dollars to pay for an image on a canvas that has less than one hundred dollars in the actual materials. They also have a preoccupation with what they call *selfies*: taking images of themselves for others to see.

Each of their images is a static story. They take thousands of images with miniscule differences and rapidly flash them in sequence, which gives the impression of movement. They sit for hours watching these rapidly moving images tell stories. Not only do they invest much of their life watching these rapidly moving images, they even respond *emotionally* to them. They're just images, and yet they cry, they laugh, they get mad or sad, just by observing them.

There appears to be something residing deep within the soul of these creatures that craves the viewing and making of images. It is as though they, and they alone out of all the species, were designed to be image-reflectors.

Storytelling is verbal imagery and it connects with us at the deepest level. Those leaders that develop this ability to tether people to significance through storytelling will have a great advantage in the conceptual age that we are entering.

Summary—Here are the building blocks and best practices that will prepare you for tomorrow's leadership challenges.

- Review the primary reasons that communication breaks down in the workplace today. Identify the one you struggle with the most and draft three personal-development suggestions that will help you minimize that specific breakdown.
- Review the list of nuanced reasons that we don't listen and check three that you are most inclined to use.
- Try a video selfie by the end of next month.
- Review the list of ten ways in which you can develop your verbal credibility and select three that you will start implementing today.
- Start using stories and images to gain buy-in. Start small but start. If you struggle with this, then get some ideas from the natural storyteller in your work environment. Every place seems to have one.
- Work on your *digital flash*.

CHAPTER 13

Meetings. Really?

Quit taking minutes and stealing hours.

People who enjoy meetings
should not be in charge of anything.
—Thomas Sowell

Root canals can seem fun… compared to the tedious meeting you just endured, again. You walk out with an equally frustrated colleague and ask, "Now, exactly what are we supposed to be doing?" or "When is it to be done by?" Ironically, the primary intent of a meeting is to convey what we are *supposed to be doing*. Meetings, in many organizations, have become the place where we take minutes and steal hours.

As a member of tomorrow's leaders, you need to elevate your understanding of the value of effective meetings, as well as of the adverse impact of ineffective meetings, to your career. Obviously, as you increase your meeting-leadership skills, your organization will reap the benefits. However, this chapter is solely focused on equipping you for career advancement.

In a nutshell, meetings are microcosms of your leadership macrocosm. Your team will subconsciously draw conclusions about your expectations as a leader by the way you lead your meetings.

I was working as a consultant with a newly arrived leader who set out to shift the organization from a less-structured culture to a more-structured culture. Over time, the performance outcomes had slipped, in large part due to a lax culture where tardiness had become embedded. Tardiness for showing up on time, for returning from breaks and lunch, for completing project reports, etc. A component of this goal was to tighten up the way meetings were conducted, including a firm start time. We set forth a plan, which included an educational meeting to launch the initiative, along with the time schedule for when it would start.

The new leader showed up late to the meeting! Worse yet, she was oblivious to the cognitive dissonance that she created. She saw the need to create a more-structured culture but didn't connect it to the less-structured meeting that she was leading. Unlike many similar stories, this one ended well. This incident became a commanding instructional moment and she went on to successfully lead her initiative.

How you lead meetings will subconsciously convey how you lead. Effective meeting management is worth your time investment.

Here Is What You Are Up Against

Let's take on some of the more common challenges that leaders face when it comes to meeting management.

Tardy Participants. First, I didn't say attendees. Use the word participant. It conveys your expectations regarding their role. Attendees show up but participants engage.

You started your meeting exactly at 10:00 a.m.—when you said you would. You are determined to establish the fact that you believe your own words, so you start the meeting on time. However, the participants slowly filter in for the next ten minutes. How will you handle this? Well, here is how you don't want to handle it: You don't want to wait until everyone gets there. You don't want to start on time and then repeat the first ten minutes after everyone is there. If you do this, then you are minimizing those who showed up on time and excusing those who were tardy. You also don't want to allow the tardy participants to interrupt or distract your meeting when they show up. Just ignore the "better late than never" attempts at humor. Don't even look in their direction or pause; just keep going as if they weren't even there. If they ask a question that was addressed in the first ten minutes, then respectfully ask them to see you after the meeting, rather than take the time of their colleagues.

Just a couple of caveats. First, some people come late to meetings because they have a solid reason. Assume that to be the case unless you know otherwise. However, keep in mind, there is a substantial difference between a reason and an excuse. An excuse is a lie stuffed in the skin of a reason. You want to give the benefit of the doubt, but you don't want to be gullible, and therefore manipulatable. Second, some cultures are more relaxed, and should be. Cultures that have high levels of creativity tend to perform better in a less-structured environment. Adapt your expectations and practices accordingly.

<u>Solutions</u>

- Start your meetings on time. Your tardiness encourages their tardiness and it removes your verbal credibility when you try to hold them accountable.
- Lock the door. The noise of fingernails scratching on the door will subside over time. Trust me, you only have to do this two consecutive times and they will start showing up early.
- Educate them—first. Don't lock the door or execute any drastic measures before you inform them first of both your precise expectation, and of the date on which it will start.
- Start off-hours. Most meetings start at the top or the bottom of the hour; 9:00 a.m. or 1:30 p.m. In many cultures, 10:00 a.m. means 10:00-ish. Try starting your meetings at 9:50 a.m. instead of 10:00 a.m., or 3:15 p.m. instead of 3:00 p.m. Anytime you break down a measurement of time into the next smaller unit of measurement, you subtly raise the perception of value. When you say 3:15, you convey that you are interested in minutes, not just hours.

Interrupter. They can't seem to stop themselves. They continually inject their voice by interrupting others. It's not only annoying, but your team is starting to question your ability to conduct a civil meeting. How do you handle this?

<u>Solutions</u>

- *Understand interrupters.* This isn't a speech or grammar problem. People invariably interpret the interrupter as a person saying that their voice is more important than the one they are interrupting. This is one of the reasons we hate to be interrupted.

- *Educate.* Start your meeting with a basic ground rule by tethering them to significance. "Because everyone's voice matters, every voice will speak one at a time."

- *Enforce.* It is not likely that your ground rule will prevent the interrupter from interrupting, but it will construct a platform of authority for you to address it when it occurs, and it will also bring the rest of the team to your side. The reason that people interrupt is because it works. We tend to stop talking and give the interrupter our attention when they interrupt. Be prepared to interrupt the interrupter. When he inserts his voice, turn your full attention to the person that was interrupted and say, "You were saying...." You can do it! If you consistently follow these steps, you will be amazed at how quickly the interrupter gets the picture, and how much your respect will grow in the eyes of your team.

Verbal narcissist. There must be some unwritten rule in many of our organizations that a meeting has to have a verbal narcissist. They just keep talking, seemingly oblivious that their words are now starting to work against them. This can be a tough one for a new leader.

<u>Solutions</u>

- *Educate.* Again, lay out the ground rule at the beginning of a meeting by tethering to significance. "Because every voice matters, we want to give every voice an opportunity."

- *One-on-one.* Depending on your rapport with the employee, it may prove beneficial for you to speak with the individual outside of the meeting. You might want to approach it like this, "Your voice matters. However, are you aware that at times you soften the impact of your words with lengthy explanations? You can actually ratchet up the power of your words by economizing them."

- *Time-keeper.* Assign someone the role of timekeeper and predesignate how long a person can speak. Give the timekeeper total authority to announce the time remaining—"You have thirty seconds." This is an especially good tool if the verbal narcissist happens to be higher on the org chart. It's best if that individual is informed before the meeting of your intent, and if you include it in your ground rules at the beginning of the meeting.

- *Precise question.* This may seem trivial but it's not. The verbal narcissist just came up for air. You step in and ask, "Are there any other ideas?" The verbal narcissist assumes from your question that you want him to keep talking, so they start in again. Everyone is chagrined. Instead of asking, "Are there any other ideas?" ask, "Does anyone else have an idea?" That nuanced shift separates speakers from speakers, rather than ideas from ideas.

Intimidator. You are in a brainstorming session and you know there are some ideas out there that are not coming forward because of the presence of an intimidator. This intimidator may simply be someone with an elevated position who tends to stymie a sense of openness; or it may be an actual bully whose revenge others don't want to contend with. Regardless, how do you deal with this intimidation factor, intended or not?

<u>Solutions</u>

- *Act.* You simply cannot let this continue, otherwise you lose control of the meeting, and the whole concept of transparency begins to wither. Remember, silence on your part will be perceived as approval.
- *Don't out a colleague.* It may be tempting to call on a colleague who has a great idea, but it goes up against the bully, and they do not want to be exposed. Your good intention of valuing their voice and including them may bring them long-term consequences.
- *Mutual and anonymous opportunity.* The bully's loud opinion has been met with silence. You know there are competing views, but no one wants to go up against the bully. Pass out a blank sheet of paper to everyone with the following instruction. "Consider the last idea (bully's idea). On one side of your paper, give me three reasons that it will succeed if it goes forward and on the opposite side, give me three reasons it will fail if it goes forward." Have them pass their anonymous papers to you. This gives everyone the anonymous freedom to express their views and it forces everyone to become the devil's advocate to their own views.

Here Is What You Need to Do

This is not an attempt to teach an exhaustive lesson on meeting management, but rather a crisp list of best practices for tomorrow's leaders.

Tether to Significance. We want better. Deep inside the DNA of humans is the desire for better. We want better living conditions, better relationships, better income, etc. No one wants worse. Along with this quest for better is the connection with meaning. Even if we don't succeed with a goal, both the attempt and struggles to achieve generate tethers to significance. We don't want to waste our time or effort. Following are the three questions that you want to attach to each item on the meeting's agenda.

Here is the scenario—you have just discussed an item on the agenda. You need to get in the habit of answering the following three questions before moving to the next item.

1. *Description: Now that we have discussed it, what exactly is to be done?* Be specific. If the item is now dead, then that action has already happened; if so, say so. Make certain that everyone knows that it's off the table.
2. *Deadline: When is it to be done by?* Avoid answering with time frames like two weeks or one month. Use specific dates like August 1. People often forget when the original meeting was held, so don't make them do extra math.
3. *Accountability: Who is responsible?* Each item needs a name associated with the next action. I call them the baton carrier. It may not be the person who is ultimately responsible for the initiative, but it is the person who is responsible for taking it to the next step.

To solidify this in your culture, consistently answer these three questions for each item in each meeting. Also, be sure to address the answers for each of the three questions when reviewing the last meeting. This is your accountability connection.

Teach Learning Bursts. Take five to ten minutes and teach your team one idea, skill, trait, etc., that will help advance their careers or help them professionally. It's a great way to address a sensitive subject when it's not currently causing an issue.

For example, you could teach the difference between *acceptance* and *agreement*. It's easy for some people to easily get offended when someone contradicts their idea. They can turn quiet and withdraw; they take their verbal toys and go home. Others sound like they are attacking the person when they are simply disagreeing with their idea.

Teach that agreement means recognizing the value of the *idea.*

Teach that acceptance means recognizing the value of the *individual.*

To the offended hearer—teach them that their ideas are to be inserted into the marketplace of ideas, for scrutiny. Some will disagree with the idea, but that doesn't mean they are devaluing the individual.

To the offending speaker—teach them to go after the idea without going after the individual.

Gather Feedback. Good leaders don't want feedback; they crave it. Look for indications of how well you are leading your meetings.

- Watercooler meetings. If your team is holding a second meeting at the watercooler after your meeting is over, then you may be having a problem with openness. As painful as it is, you need your team to have the freedom to speak openly in your meetings.
- Feedback cards. Occasionally, hand out blank index cards, or even Post-it Notes, to each participant and have them anonymously answer one question with a one-word answer. "Was my time wasted in this meeting?" If you start to see an uncomfortable number of "yesses" then you can take it to the next level of feedback. Periodically using the feedback cards should help you keep your finger on the pulse of your meeting-management skills.
- Feedback. Use the "Please start, please stop, and please continue" statements. For more information refer to *Solicit feedback from your team* in chapter 4.

Stand-up meetings. If you find your meetings are lacking focus and the small talk is taking over, try stand-up meetings. People are inclined to stay on subject when they stand.

Pass the verbal baton. This is a common failure. People failed to consider that conclusions were made in the meeting that affect people outside the meeting, and yet no plan was developed to inform them. Develop the habit of asking "Who else needs to know?" You may find that adding the question at the bottom of your agenda may go a long way to tasking the baton carriers—the people who will be communicating the conclusions.

Finger on the pulse. Teams, like people, have ups and downs. There are some meetings in which you may want to jump right into business, and others in which you may want to give your team some time for small talk. Keep your finger on the pulse of your team. Do they need to celebrate; are they discouraged; are they challenged; are they confused? Avoid leading your meetings as though they are detached from the culture at large.

Use humor. Humor can be one of those wonderful, terrible things. There are times that humor may be your best team-building tool and stress reliever. However, you need to be careful with humor. There are several people that are seeking employment elsewhere due to poor judgment in humor. The safest subject is yourself. We are attracted to people who use self-deprecating humor. If you aren't one inclined to humor, almost certainly there are others on your team that would gladly fill that role. Use them. Just a caution, however: Some people are humor-free, some people have a great sense of humor, and some people are humor-free but think they have a great sense of humor. Know the difference.

Summary—Here are the building blocks and best practices that will prepare you for tomorrow's leadership challenges.

- Ask yourself, "What conclusions would I draw about my leadership in general if I were able to covertly sit in on a meeting that I was leading."
- After your next meeting, ask yourself if interrupters were gaining unearned audiences or if they were managed well.
- Try using the three questions (description, deadline, and accountability) for each agenda item at your next meeting.
- Begin using Learning Bursts in your meetings. Start with the acceptance-agreement distinction.
- Use the Feedback Card idea following your next large meeting.

CHAPTER 14

Making Peace with Conflict

How to win the person and not just the point.

It is one thing to show a man that he is in error,
and another to put him in possession of truth.
—JOHN LOCKE

Not again! Why can't people just play nice together? Conflict is so frustrating, not to mention demoralizing, and it thwarts performance outcomes.

It might surprise you that the place to start with conflict management is here: *not all conflict is bad.* It can be used to identify root causes of problems, to surface underlying issues, to refine good ideas, and to strengthen relationships, if it is handled correctly. Just because it's uncomfortable doesn't mean that it's bad. (More on this in chapter 17.) It is disconcerting to see the direction that culture is headed in this regard. The whole idea that someone may be offended by words, and that therefore we ought to silence those words, when pushed to the extreme means that no one should be speaking. It's inevitable that ideas generate friction. Critical thinking cannot survive if speech is silenced when someone is offended. We need to make peace with conflict.

However, much of the conflict in the work environment today, like in society at large, is unhealthy and unnecessary. That is where our focus resides in this chapter.

Every senior leader has taken conflict-management training, or so it seems. Yet, unhealthy conflicts flourish. Puzzling. It appears to me that many have attended the *Jerry Springer School of Conflict Management.*

In a previous lifetime, I taught conflict-management skills in an open setting where organizations sent their leaders, aspiring and seasoned, to learn how to deal with conflict. It was readily apparent that many of these attendees had very little interest in managing conflict, let alone resolving conflict. Some even cherished the prized skill of conflict-nurturing. The chances of those participants developing conflict management skills was not encouraging. No leader can effectively traffic in unexperienced truth, for any length of time.

Common Misdiagnosis Trap

Let's start with a caution. Probably the most common explanation for conflict involving two people is *personality conflict*. It seems to be the default diagnosis. Like all diagnoses, if it's incorrect, then the corrective measures will be flawed.

Personality conflict—let's explore it. It is believed that no one can voluntarily change their personality, so when the diagnosis of personality conflict is declared, it's also saying that nothing can be done about it. Without realizing it, this diagnosis unjustly traps people. They think they have the answer, but the answer provides no solution. Sure, there are people who have personalities that make it difficult for them to get along with other personalities—I agree. To some extent, we all have that. But can you picture two people that, personality-wise, should be two peas in a pod, and yet you can't find a pod big enough for them? It is possible that they may have even been BFFs for a period, but no more. And, can you also picture two people that have personalities that should repel each other, but they choose to get along, and do so very well? There is a path forward to peace, so when we declare personality conflict, we are incarcerating people to their own well-lit prison. An answer without a solution is a flawed diagnosis.

You Have Options

I see three basic options when approaching conflict. I call it the PRM approach.

1. *Prevention*: We just don't want to rock the boat, so we end up ignoring the potential conflict. We just wish it into non-existence. It rarely works. The best

time to address conflict is before it blossoms. Managing agreement is preferable to managing conflict. When the cracks of conflict first emerge, reemphasize the commonalities that your team has. They might be common goals, history, values, ideals, relationships, benefits, etc. If your common ground is solid, then you have a platform to manage agreement. Failure to do so puts you in a position where conflict starts managing you.

So, how does tomorrow's leader prevent it?

- Believe that every person has intrinsic value.
- Live in truth. Be yourself.
- Listen authentically.
- Prefer others above yourself.
- Encourage openness.
- Address problems decisively.
- Be available.
- Encourage appropriate humor.
- Be mature. (Maturity is the ability to handle immaturity in others.)
- Follow up.
- Deflect praise to others.
- Lead selflessly.

2. *Resolution*: Peace is not the cessation of fighting. Peace is when two conflicting entities choose to be on the same side. Think how this works on the relationship level. There's a difference between an *apology* and asking for *forgiveness*. If your child inadvertently spills their milk, then an apology is in order—"I'm sorry." But if your child punches the neighbor kid in the nose, or they steal candy from the local market, or they lie to their teacher, these actions require more than an apology. They require a request for forgiveness. If it's a mistake, an apology will suffice. However, if there is an immoral intent, then a request for forgiveness is in order.

Listen to the cacophony of apologies from your politicians and consider how ineffective they are. Apologies express emotions but they don't put two parties on the same side. Apologizing for an immoral act (lying, cheating, stealing, etc.) is an attempt to diminish the gravity of the act; but authentically asking for forgiveness, which requires a response from the aggrieved, most often results in peace—that is, two choosing to be on the same side. Apologies flourish in our culture, but peace doesn't. Maybe it's time to dust off that old word and concept: forgiveness.

3. *Management*: In World War II, the US (Allies) fought the Germans and the Japanese. Today we have peace with those great nations. We are on the same side. During the Korean war, the US (UN) fought North Korea, which ended in a truce, not peace. There is just a temporary cessation in open hostilities. Today we are still trying to manage the conflict with North Korea. When resolution is not availed of, then we must resort to managing conflict.

De-escalating the Conversation

Did you ever wish you could just calmly deal with a conversation that is quickly spinning out of control? Your amygdala is starting to flash, and you can feel yourself being emotionally sucked into the conversation that is escalating in tension and volume. You sense that it's not going to end well, but you don't know how to get out of it, let alone de-escalate it.

Apartment dwellers know what I'm talking about. The neighbors are at it again. They're going at each other over some trivial issue and neither of them seems to know how to get a handle on the conflict. The more they talk, the more upset they get. OK, we all know what I am talking about, not just apartment dwellers.

Here is your seven-step plan to de-escalate the conversation.

1. *Refresh your perspective.* Maturity is the ability to handle immaturity in others. You are not likely to win debate points once the conversation reaches a certain temperature. This conversation needs an adult participant. You, as the leader, are that adult. Place a higher priority on handling the conflict than on proving yourself right.
2. *Avoid interrupting.* When we interrupt, we poke their amygdala and the conversational temperature rises. Be careful not to work against yourself.
3. *Avoid absolutes.* When we are distraught, we lean on absolutes like "you always" and "you never." Absolutes stimulate more frustration, are rarely true, and never help us win the argument.
4. *Take ownership for your words.* This is a subtle but significant way to help you guide a conversation to a constructive outcome. An argument often centers around what someone said or didn't say. Take ownership for your words. Try this. Instead of saying "*You said* you were going to make the phone call," try "*I understood you to say* that you were going to make the phone call." Shifting from "you said" to "I understood you to say" is a nuanced shift in the

ownership of words. You can argue about what someone said, and we often do, but you can't argue about what someone heard. Leverage this to your advantage.

I like watching the talking heads on TV, or online, unknowingly conflate words. Many within our culture have a decreasing interest in the precise meaning of words, which puts us at a disadvantage on so many different levels. Conflict resolution is one of those. Take the two words "imply" and "infer" for instance. It is not infrequent that you hear a frustrated person in a heated conversation start their sentence with "You inferred..." The precise meaning of the two words is an opposite. A speaker cannot infer, and a hearer cannot imply. Only speakers can imply and only hearers can infer. It is the difference between throwing a ball and catching a ball. Implying is like throwing the ball, inferring is like catching the ball. When you say, "I understood you to say," you are inferring and taking ownership for what you heard, not what they said.

5. *Lower your volume.* In these last three points, you are working against human nature as it is displayed in a heated conversation. Take another lesson from your noisy neighbors. The more frustrated they get, the *louder* the conversation. Work against this impulse. The louder they get, the more you need to retain a lower, but consistent volume.

6. *Slow your cadence.* As your neighbors get more frustrated, the *faster* they talk. Slow your cadence down. Speak with a measured and controlled pace.

7. *Enlarge the gap.* As your neighbors get more frustrated, the more they start talking over each other. Determine to wait an elongated second to start talking after they have finished.

Where Is That Conflict Coming From?

At some point in your career, you will have someone who simply can't stand you. This is troubling to some leaders, especially emerging leaders. They set out to fix it. They give this person extra effort. They listen more attentively, they laugh harder at their jokes, and give them favored assignments; but all to no avail.

If you find yourself in this position, zoom out and take a fresh, evaluative look and ask, "Where is the conflict coming from?" To answer the question correctly, ask a series of telescoping questions.

- *Is their conflict just with me?* If it is just between the two of you, then you have a clear context in which to resolve or manage the conflict. It's just the two of you.
- *Is their conflict with me and the team?* Now the context is a little larger. It involves more people, so it's not likely that this conflict can be resolved simply between the two of you. You now have less to work with, because you have more people to work with.
- *Is their conflict with me, the team, and the organization?* It may be that you are the *focus* of their frustration, but that doesn't mean that you are the *cause* of the conflict. It may have nothing to do with you other than the fact that you are the face of the organization to them. When this is the case, you aren't going to resolve the conflict by personal attempts to win them over. Your role in the resolution will be as a representative of the organization, not as an individual.
- *Is their conflict with me, the team, the organization, and the rest of the world?* It is not likely that you, in the role of supervisor, will be able to resolve this conflict. Every person can change, but it isn't likely that the supervisor will be that agent of change.

Winners Start at the Bottom

You got that promotion! You decide to celebrate with a nice steak dinner. You go to your favorite restaurant and you order your steak well done. However, the waiter returns with your steak barely cooked instead of well done. I mean blood-red rare. The description where I come from is, "I have seen cows injured worse than this, and they recovered." Frustrating. You can feel your amygdala start to flash.

So how do you handle this aggravating situation in such a way as to get your steak cooked the way you want it and yet not create unnecessary conflict?

There are essentially three approaches.

1. *Aggressive.* This option makes you feel good, and everybody else feel bad. Typically, the aggressive person will use volume, anger, and accusation to get the job done. They go after the waiter regardless of whether it was his fault or not. The aggressive person thinks they are in control, when they obviously are not. If you have ever worked in a restaurant, you know this may not end

well for the customer and his steak. Just saying. The aggressive person is identified as one who risks solution while pursuing blame.

2. *Passive*. This option goes the other direction. The passive person can handle this steak debacle in two different ways. Some passive customers will simply not eat it and ask for a to-go container. Other passive customers will take the opposite approach and eat it. They're thinking that if they're paying for it, then it's going down the chute. Even though the aggressive and passive person handle the situation with opposite responses, they both do it for the same reason. The passive person is identified as one who risks non-solution while preventing conflict. Ironically, both the aggressive and passive person may be taking their opposite approach because they have the same focus—self. The aggressive person displays his self-focus by demanding that he get his way. The passive person, on the other hand, displays his self-focus by trying to control what people think of him.

3. *Assertive*. The assertive person is identified as one who goes after solution, while minimizing conflict. I encourage you to start at the bottom of the verbal ladder and work up, but only as needed. Did you ever have someone explode at you in a burst of anger, and then, during the ridiculous tirade, catch themselves? They suddenly realize that they are coming across as a certified kook; so, they turned sweet on you. How well does that work? Not at all! Remember, you can always go up the verbal ladder, but you can't come down.

   Therefore, you may want to consider starting with a question, even when you're annoyed. "Do you remember how I ordered that steak?" If this waiter is worth his weight in sawdust, he will take ownership for the steak and make it happen. He doesn't feel like he has been blamed, the neighboring customers don't have their evening ruined, you aren't all stressed out, and you get your steak properly cooked—without any unrequested additives! But, if the waiter doesn't cooperate, you can always ratchet up your approach, including a conversation with the manager. In potentially heated situations, use only the minimum amount of verbal ammunition that the situation calls for.

Make the Position Talk

As a newly appointed leader, you are ready to make a difference. One of the first areas of focus is your employees' performance. You do a great job of monitoring their performance. You have come to realize early on that if you don't monitor it, you can't measure it, and if you can't measure it, you can't manage it. So, like a responsible leader, you sit down with your employee with a clear understanding of their past performance and an equally clear understanding of what your expectations are. You begin to convey those expectations with phrases that start with, "I need for you to…" or "I want you to…" You may be laying a foundation of conflict between you and your employee without even realizing it. You're building a tension point between you and the employee.

Try this instead. Make the position talk. Convey your expectations through the language of the position's requirements. If you do this, you shift the tension points away from you to them now residing between the employee and the position, enabling you to partner with your employee in their effort to achieve the position's requirements (your expectations). Even though you're accountable for their performance, you want them to believe that you're on their side as they achieve. Just a tip—it works much better if you actually are on their side!

Popeye Was Wrong

It's not clear to me why we thought it was amusing, but Popeye the Sailor Man was noted for proclaiming, "I yam what I yam and that's all what I yam." In his inimitable way, he was conveying that what you see is what you get. Although there are some admirable qualities to that statement surrounding authenticity, there is an entrapping principle as well. If a leader takes the position of approaching every person and every conversation with an inflexible communication approach, then conflicts will inevitably follow in their wake. Hiding behind "I yam what I yam" is not the perspective, or practice, of conflict-resolution leaders. The conflict-resolution leader possesses the insight to discern people and circumstances, and the courageous humility to modify their communication approach accordingly.

My dad had numerous opportunities to observe his six kids deal with sibling conflicts. I can recall him teaching, "Don't just try to win the point; try to win the person." I took that sage insight and developed it into the PACE Adaptation Quadrant, which we'll take a look at in a moment.

Almost every conversation has *a point*. The point may be informing, selling, information gathering, negotiating, correcting, problem solving, instructing, etc. It's the reason for which the conversation exists. Every conversation has two or more people. Without realizing it, we make value judgments in the moment, regarding both the *point* and the *person*. The conflict-resolution leader recognizes both of these values and modifies their communication approach based upon the higher priority of the two.

Just to be clear: When you consider the value of the person in the PACE model, you are *not* referring to the intrinsic value of the person, but to the relational value of the person. Every person has the same intrinsic value, but not every person has the same relational value. Are your kids more valuable to you than your neighbors' kids are? Of course they are. However, because your kids have a greater relational value to you than your neighbors' kids, that does not mean they have a greater intrinsic value than your neighbors' kids.

When the PACE model compares or contrasts the value of the point to the value of the *person*, it's referring to that person's relationship to you. (See Exhibit 14. 1.)

The value of the person's relationship to you is indicated by the vertical arrow on the left. The higher the value of the relationship, the more influence that relationship will have in determining our best communication approach. We want to win them. The lower the value of the person's relationship, the less emphasis we will invest in winning that person.

The tension points come when considering the value of the point. The higher the value of the point, as indicated by the horizontal arrow on the bottom, the more we want to win it. The lower the value of the point, the less important it is for us to win it. The challenge is to identify and consider the value of the person (relationship) in comparison to the value of the point, and then to determine how to best approach the conversation. This is where PACE will help us.

Exhibit 14.1.

PACE© - **Adaptation Quadrant**

	THE POINT — LOSE	THE POINT — WIN
WIN — THE PERSON	1. *P*assive Win the PERSON Lose the POINT	3. *C*ollaborative Win the PERSON Win the POINT
THE PERSON	4. *E*vasive Lose the PERSON Lose the POINT	2. *A*ggressive Lose the PERSON Win the POINT

LOSE   **THE POINT**   WIN

Exhibit 14. 1.

<u>Quadrant #1. **Passive**</u>. *Win the PERSON: Lose the POINT*. This quadrant represents a high-value relationship that we want to win. We want this relationship protected, encouraged, and deepened. The point is on the other end. It's a low-value point; especially when compared to the value of the person (relationship).

Your high-value client conveys in an email that she would like to meet you next Thursday at 3:30 p.m. in her office. You show up at 3:20 p.m. and you're met with an already irritated high-value client. She greets you with, "Where have you been for the last twenty minutes?" She's obviously mistaken about the meeting time. Right here is where you decide how you will respond. Is the value of the point (confusion about the meeting time) more or less important than the value of the person (relationship: high-value client)? We all know people who immediately elevate the value of the point at the expense of the person. They so zealously set out to prove they are correct with their point, that they end up losing the person. We all know the person who must win every argument that they are in. If you watch that person carefully, you will note that they have numerous fractured relationships in their wake; but they won the point!

Courageously adapt your communication strategy and take the Passive approach. It's more important for you to protect and encourage this relationship than to prove that you were right.

Let me encourage you as a parent to take note of this quadrant. This is one of my biggest regrets as a parent. In that moment of frustration with my kids, I lost sight of the high value of my kids, in relationship to the relatively lower value of the point. In that moment, the point became more important than my kid. The values were blurred because of my Popeye approach. I momentarily lost sight of the fact that there are only four kids in the world that can call me "Dad." Consider *both* values and then form your communication approach.

<u>Quadrant #2. **Aggressive**</u>. *Win the POINT: Lose the PERSON*. In this scenario, the opposite is true. The value of the person (relationship) is low, while the value of the point is high.

You tell your high school senior that you will buy her a used car at graduation, if she graduates on the honor roll. She does, and so you do. The two of you go down to the local "lemon orchard" and look at used cars. You converse with the sales rep about a specific vehicle. The value of the point (price of the car) is relatively high, especially in relationship to the value of the person (relationship: car sales rep). You want to take a more aggressive approach to communication even though it may not win you relationship points with the sales rep.

If that sales rep is savvy, and they often are, they will try to convince you that they're your buddy. They're on your side. They will talk with their manager on your behalf, to see if he would begrudgingly throw in that extra package just for you. Why? Because they're trying to soften your point (price of the car), by convincing you that they have a special relationship with you. Buy the car, not the speech. I'm not suggesting that you mistreat the sales rep, or even become rude; but you don't want that relationship to influence the value of your point (price of the car).

<u>Quadrant #3</u>. **Collaborative.** *Win the PERSON: Win the POINT.* This is the tough one. You can't teach, or talk about, communication without saying "win/win" at some point, so here it is. This is where you have both a high-value point and a high-value person (relationship). To be candid, this looks better in a PowerPoint slide than it does in real life. It can be a serious challenge choosing the collaborative approach because it requires a list of skills and traits like listening, negotiating, questioning, compromising, and persistence, not to mention a large dose of patience.

<u>Quadrant #4</u>. **Evasive**. *Lose the PERSON: Lose the POINT.* This is the easy one, but the worst option. This is where you have encountered a person that you would rather avoid and be willing to give up the point because they're so toxic. You may have to end up here, but you don't ever want to start here.

Here's an extreme illustration: You tell your ten-year-old daughter who loves puppies that if some strange guy stops and shows you a picture of his lost puppy, and he wants you to get in his pickup truck to help you find that lost puppy—don't! You tell her to run, scream, kick, throw a rock through his window, but do not get in that vehicle. In this scenario, you don't care about that person (relationship: potential pedophile), and you don't care about the point (lost puppy). You teach your kids to consider the value of the person (relationship) no matter how attractive that point may be in the moment. This is the time to evade.

Conclusion: Popeye didn't get it. Do you?

*Pre*conversation *adapting:* Most of us have a natural propensity to one of these four approaches. Can you identify which of the four you are most inclined to lean toward? My default approach is obvious: Aggressive. When I have lazily defaulted to my "Popeye approach," I ended up injuring people whom I care deeply about, with words. However, just knowing that there are other communication options to choose from helps minimize my "Popeye" damage. I can select another approach based on the value of the person and the value of the point.

If you know your propensity, especially if it's a strong propensity, you have an advantage. By default, we lean on our "Popeye approach" when we're stressed out, fatigued, or apathetic. Knowing this to be true can help us quickly identify the value of the other approaches, when to consider using them, and how to adapt.

Mid-*conversation adapting*: Just a caution: Each approach has a strength to it, but each one also has an inherent weakness. Take the Collaborative approach in quadrant #2—win the person, win the point. It sounds good, but it can be done to an excess, which generates pushback. Have you ever been in a meeting where a debate has escalated into a conflict? The leader, by default takes the "Popeye Collaborative approach" and wants everyone to just get along. They push for the two sides to come together for a common outcome, but without success. To the team, it begins to feel exhausting and frustrating. It feels like the leader is manipulating them into a position that they can't embrace. It has now become tedious, laborious, and time-consuming. By the end, the two sides have come to agree on one thing: They just want the leader to simply make "the call."

It is essential for you to be able to sense, in mid-conversation, when your existing communication approach is not working, and how to adapt to another approach.

Summary—Here are the building blocks and best practices that will prepare you for tomorrow's leadership challenges.

- Ask yourself what you can do to help build a conflict-prevention culture.
- Review the last three work-related conflicts. Could you have done anything differently to resolve those conflicts, or even prevent them?
- Review the seven steps to de-escalate a conversation and identify the one(s) that you will start to regularly implement.
- Try making the position talk in your next employee development session.
- Review the section on winning the person and winning the point, as well as the PACE Adaptation Quadrant (see Exhibit 14. 1.). Engage in a conversation from one of those perspectives.

CHAPTER 15

Untidy Organizational Skills

The ability to retrieve.

> Order is the sanity of the mind, the health of the body,
> the peace of the city, the security of the state.
> Like beams in a house or bones to a body,
> so is order to all things.
> —ROBERT SOUTHEY

Americans like stuff. Lots of stuff. There's a saying: *The American dream is buying things we don't need, with money we don't have, to impress people we don't like.* Stuff has made our houses full—and stressful. It isn't enough that our land is littered with stores where we can buy more stuff, but we've now built between 45,000 and 52,000 self-storage units to store the stuff that we bought from stores. There are twice as many self-storage units as there are Starbucks and McDonald's—combined[1,35] In 2015, the US self-storage industry generated less than one billion dollars. By 2018 it had grown to over five billion dollars![2] Why? Because we have so much stuff that we can't get our cars in our garages. In almost half of the houses in the US we can't get a car in the garage because it's full of stored stuff. And stored stuff has a cost.

Cost of Clutter

On the surface, our stuff may seem benign. It just passively sits there waiting for the next time we need it. Sometimes that's the case, but more frequently it's not. Consider how, and how much, disorganized stuff costs you. This is the very fuel that has propelled the Minimalist Movement with such stunning growth within one of the most materialistic cultures.

My time. How much time do you waste looking for that lost __________ (fill in the blank)? The more stuff we have, the more time we waste trying to find it—not to mention the time spent replacing it. Then we spend even more time finding a new storage space for the new item we purchased to replace the item that's sitting somewhere in our previously stored stuff. We can waste even more time searching to locate that item that we stored for years, only to discover that time has rendered it obsolete; and so we take more time to discard it and to buy an updated replacement item.

My money. I'm talking real money here. One of the prime reasons we store stuff is because we don't want to buy another one. It seems to make sense; but all too frequently we are selling ourselves a convincing lie. The items in your house have a cost; in fact, different costs. The same is true in any organization. The item can deteriorate, depreciate, get bruised by neighboring stuff, and/or become obsolete. It must be protected from the elements and insured, and it may even be taxed.

My relationships. Money, for the most part, is a symbol of stuff. As a counselor for many years, I can tell you that the most common cause of marital strife is money. The adage "fences make the best neighbors" rings true because it prevents friction over stuff. Stuff not only fractures marriages, but it can destroy any familial relationship. Following death, the will is read. All too frequently, where there is a will, there is a war.

My health. We waste our health in midlife attempting to gain our wealth, and then waste our wealth in later life attempting to regain our health. Accumulating, protecting, insuring, and maintaining our stuff can take a toll on our health.

I Am a Rat

A pack rat that is. More specifically, a recovering pack rat. My nice, carless garage was full of stuff. Good stuff, accumulated stuff, valuable stuff, and stuff I couldn't do without. It had become an increasingly contentious issue between my wife and me. One day, upon returning from a business trip, I opened the garage door to find a completely bare-naked garage staring back at me. Only a few items remained. In a moment of justifiable frustration, Marilyn and my two sons decided to "clean out" my garage for me and dumped everything except a few items. I admit it, Marilyn became the focal point of my aggressive approach to communication. The sad reality is this: Since that day, on only *one* occasion did I ever need something that they threw away, and that one item cost less than twenty dollars. Marilyn's aggravating lesson taught me to love the exhilaration of open and usable space over the love of stuff. Love takes many forms, and one of those is "desiring the best for someone and doing all within my power to bring it to pass." She made me realize how much my stuff cost me in time, money, and in our relationship. Ironically, the roles seem to have mildly reversed in the subsequent years. My shop is invigoratingly open, with only a few needed tools, while my wife's walk-in closet...never mind.

De-Cluttering Strategy

So we need to de-clutter; but what is the ongoing workable plan? Try this one. Ask yourself these six questions and in this sequence.

1. *SORT IT: What do I have?*
    Take an inventory. Stuff seems to multiply in the dark, and it's easy to lose track of what you have.
2. *CULL IT: What do I keep?*
    Prepare yourself. This is the painful step. Prepare yourself to part paths with that which fails to bring value to your life. Keep clear on what your values are. Does it have monetary value, nostalgic value, or potential value? Be realistic. A spouse can often give us some annoying help with this. Listen to them carefully.

    Prepare a place. Make provisions for the stuff you're keeping. Do you have the proper number and size of containers, the proper markers, and your favorite labeling tool? You also want to make provisions for the stuff you're culling. Will you be selling it, giving it to charity, burning it, or dumping it? Will you need a dumpster, a transporting vehicle, or manual labor? Do you know where the charity is and what its business hours are?
3. *ZONE IT: Where should I put it?*
    One of the biggest mistakes when organizing is to place items in locations based on the available space. "It would fit nicely here so I will put it here," will help you store it, but not locate it. Remember, what files are to your information, zones are to your possessions.
4. *CONTAIN IT: What should I put it in?*
    Small items are best organized when placed in a larger container. This not only helps you to locate them when needed but it also helps to prevent loss and damage.

5. *LABEL IT: How can I find it?*

    Use totes and be sure to label them. Better yet, use transparent totes with labels.

6. *ADJUST IT: How can I maintain it?*

    Organizing is not an event; it's a process. An ongoing process. The more you monitor and tweak your storage, the more you sense order.

The key that helps me with organization is to simply view it through the lens of one question: "Can it be retrieved easily by those who need to use it?" If it can, then you're organized. If it can't, you've got more organizing in front of you.

Tethering Through Organizing

Drawn by Charlotte Wipf (age 13)
One of my favorite three granddaughters!

There are some informal clubs that I call the Make Your Bed Club and the Clean Your Desk Club. I am a firm member of both. It goes like this. Before we can change the world, we need to manage our own. The world is going to change when individuals manage their own world well. When we manage our own world well, then our impact ripples outward. As we manage and improve our little world, additional peripheral opportunities will present themselves for us to do the same with. Remember: start small and work big. If you turn it on, you turn it off. If you drop it, you pick it up. If you break it, you fix it. If you open it, you close it. If you borrow it, you return it. Work on developing a sense of ownership for your sphere of influence.

Have you heard of the secret coffee cup test? It's an informal hiring assessment technique that younger managers are starting to use. This is where the manager takes the candidate on a tour of the facilities which typically includes the kitchen. They offer the candidate a cup of coffee and then return to their office at the completion of the tour. Once the interview is completed, the manager watches to see what the candidate does with their empty coffee cup. If they attempt to return the cup to the kitchen, they get hired. The hiring manager draws a conclusion that the candidate is an individual who has an attitude of ownership even in the small areas of their life, and that is quite appealing.

Think about a person whose life is coming apart at the seams. One of the first indicators is displayed right here: Their appearance and world become disheveled. Their bed remains unmade, their clothes are on the floor, their hygiene begins to slip, their car goes unmaintained. A common phrase to describe a person who is on the opposite end of this continuum is "They have it all together." It's an appropriate phrase.

Summary—Here are the building blocks and best practices that will prepare you for tomorrow's leadership challenges.

- Conduct a scan of your workspace and assess your organizational skills based on the one question, how easy is it to retrieve?
- Identify an organization-free space. It could be your email inbox, your computer files, your garage, your office, your closet, your RV, etc. Use the six-step De-Cluttering Strategy.
- Develop a learned instinct to increase your organizational influence every week. Straighten something, clean something, fix something, store something, toss something, etc.
- Teach your kids: If you dropped it, pick it up; if you broke it, fix it; if you borrowed it, return it; if you opened it, close it; and if you turned it on, turn it off.

PEER-LEADER QUOTE

Tomorrow's Leader understands the bridge between
leading change and managing operational excellence.

JEREMY LONG
Senior Manager
Sustainable Packaging
Amazon

CHAPTER 16

Customers Are Number One. It's a Lie!

You can't display what you don't possess.

If you're not serving the customer,
your job is to be serving someone who is.
—JAN CARLZON

Customers are Number One. They are the reason that organizations exist, and therefore, they are always to be first in our perspective, decisions, and behaviors. This attractive concept has been taught by customer-service trainers (myself included) for decades. We have structured systems, language, teams, strategies, etc., around the concept that customers are Number One. But it doesn't seem to work as well as we had hoped.

Customer Service Challenges

- *CSIG: Customer Service Integrity Gap.* Throughout the years, I have been invited into organizations to help them design and implement a customer-centric culture predicated on this concept, only to see their efforts frequently produce modest outcomes. Frustrating—not to mention a severe blow to money and morale.

Here is why. The organization would try to generate external relationships with customers, relationships that did not exist internally. There would be dissension within the ranks of their management about how they were to treat customers in a preferential manner. I would look up on the wall and read their Customer Service Value posters, and then look back at how they were conducting themselves internally, and then look up at the poster again, and then back at the heated discussion. I often wondered how long it had been since someone even read those customer-service values, let alone aspired to use them.

You cannot get better external customer service than that which resides internally. We simply cannot traffic in unexperienced truth for any length of time. I refer to this flawed concept as the *CSIG—Customer Service Integrity Gap*. This is the difference between how we conduct ourselves with internal customers and how we conduct ourselves with external customers. This gap creates a culture fraught with cognitive dissonance, fatigue, and frustration—not to mention relational damage with customers.

- *Static customer service.* If your customer service is not improving, then it's probably slipping. The expectations of customers in general are soaring. If we ordered a bicycle from Amazon five years ago and they informed us that it would arrive in four days, we would have been impressed. Today if we order the same bicycle from Amazon, and they tell us that it will arrive in four days, we wonder, "What in the world is their problem?" The customer service skills of tomorrow must be viewed as fluid.

- *Bottom line damage.* Consider the impact that customer service has on an entire country. France has more tourists than any other country. Spain, on the other hand, has far fewer tourists than France. In fact, they have about half the tourists that France has. However, tourists are willing to spend over two and a half times the money in Spain that they choose to spend in France.[1] The reason: Spain is known for its stellar customer service. France, not so much. France's less-than-stellar customer service has a negative financial impact on every man, woman, and child in the country, even though they may be completely unaware of it.

In a similar way, the customer service that your organization displays also has an impact in some way on every man, woman, and child affiliated with your organization, even though they may be completely unaware of it.

Customer Service Solutions

Although there is much to be considered in developing a customer-centric culture, let's not make it more difficult than it is. Here is your four-step process to overcoming the customer service challenges of tomorrow.

1. *Create and display your customer service values.* Every organization has a character, if you will. That character is formed primarily by the behavior of senior leadership, and secondly by their stated values. If patience is one of your customer service values, then it must be seen in leadership behavior, not just on the poster.

2. *Hire and promote to support those values.* I was talking with the director of training for a national retailer that is known to display a gold standard for customer service. I asked her who did the training for her company and she replied, "Our employees' parents." She went on to explain that they could train people to become CPAs, IT SMEs, buyers, etc., but that it was much more difficult to teach them to prefer others. If your values are truly valuable, then they will provide decision-making power with personnel.

3. *Gather and use customer service feedback.* I hate them too, but surveys are one way of getting valuable feedback. There are numerous other ways, but whichever feedback mechanism you select, use it. It's all too often that great feedback is gathered, but it goes no further.

4. *Train and retain to those values.* The customer service of tomorrow must be fluid, which requires nimble and courageous leaders. They need to be nimble to modify the training to exceed the customers' expectations, and they need courage to release those employees who will not support those values. This step becomes less painful if we do a great job with the first two steps.

Summary—Here are the building blocks and best practices that will prepare you for tomorrow's leadership challenges.

- Strive to treat internal customers as though they are as important as external customers.
- Ask yourself if you are doing your part to minimize the CSIG – Customer Service Integrity Gap.
- Gather customer feedback, either formal or informal, and use it to modify your personal approach to customer service.
- Know and incorporate your organization's customer service values whether anyone else does or not.

PEER-LEADER QUOTE

Tomorrow's leader is an agent of change and doesn't allow fear or unintended consequences to get in the way of achieving progress.

MARIE GAYO
President
Trident Mortgage Company
Berkshire Hathaway HomeServices Fox & Roach

CHAPTER 17

Team Building or Cat Herding

Why are we still trying to row the boat faster with the anchor out?

No one can whistle a symphony. It takes an orchestra to play it.
—H. E. Luccock

f you have ever served on a high-impact team, you know that it's a great work experience, as well as a great life experience. But why is this experience so rare when teams are so common? Why does it seem so difficult to get a group of adults moving in the same direction, and then to *keep* them moving in that direction?

The subject of team building is quite complex due to a variety of factors. It is not my intent in this chapter to explore those complexities and their correlating solutions. That is for another book. In this chapter we will focus on the narrower subject of getting people focused and motivated as a unit. This is still the major challenge for even the most complex of teams.

Let's start with a basic premise. All teams are groups but not all groups are teams. Calling your group a team doesn't make it a team. There's much more to it.

You've probably been there. On paper, your team should be high-powered, but in reality, it leans toward dysfunction. It does so because there's an under-the-surface issue. Everyone is aware that there's an under-the-surface issue, and everyone is aware that everyone is aware. Yet no one seems to have the courage to address it.

Here's what is often done. The team recognizes that they have a certain dysfunctionality and so the team leader whips out his best motivational ideas. He holds contests, hands out awards, schedules team-building retreats, and leads coerced merriment parties...but to no avail. Motivation rarely, if ever, solves problems. Adding motivational impetus is like trying to row the boat faster with the anchor still out. Team problems must be solved, not soothed.

You may have heard the story of the four guys who went golfing every Saturday. One particular Saturday, a golfer didn't return home at lunch as was his normal practice; he showed up late in the evening. His frustrated wife met him at the door and asked why he was so late. He replied with a startling story. They had just finished their tee shots on the first hole when Harry dropped dead of a heart attack. His distraught wife responded with, "That's terrible! But why are you so late?" He replied, "Do you know how long it takes to hit the ball, drag Harry; hit the ball, drag Harry...?" OK, maybe not even worth a groan, but it conveys a great point. It's quite common for teams to have an under-the-surface issue, while nobody has the courage to get out the shovel and bury Harry. They just keep trying to hit the ball and drag Harry. Tomorrow's team leaders must have the courage to bury the Harrys.

Team-Building Approach for Leaders

Tomorrow's team leader must recognize the uniqueness of the individual and be able to adapt their leadership approach accordingly. There are three basic styles of leadership to consider: the autocratic, the democratic, and the indirect. I refer to these three styles as the A-D-I Leadership Approach. There are two components that move a leader from one style to another, and those two components are *authority* and *communication* (see Exhibit 17. 1.).

Autocratic Leader. The autocratic leader is one who holds all the authority and all the communication. Their approach to team building is "my way." Sometimes they even add a navigational term as well—"or the highway." They see two entities: the boss and the non-bosses. They delegate tasks instead of outcomes because they have a lack of

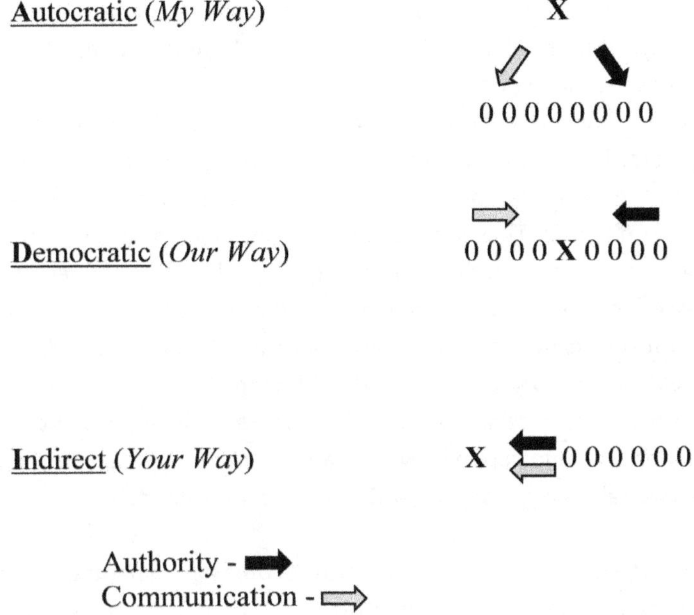

trust in their team. They also have little interest in the opinions and the perspectives of the team. The autocratic leader is often known by the following:

- *Time-debt.* Because they fail to develop their team, they end up overburdened and feeling like they owe people time from yesterday. They operate their career in time-debt.
- *Morale-busters.* When the autocratic leader is absent from the meeting, the meeting has a different atmosphere. When the autocratic leader is on vacation, the work environment has a breath of fresh air.
- *Communication-dispensers.* When the autocratic leader wants your opinion, they will tell you what it is.

Both authority and communication flow from the autocratic leader down to the team.

Democratic Leader. The democratic leader has a different perspective and therefore a different approach. This leader sees herself as part of the team. She views the team as a group of peers and approaches the work outcomes through the lens of doing things "our way." As a result, she is secure enough to share her authority with her team. They are involved in solving problems and setting goals. They are also an integral part of the communication flow. They contribute ideas, and they have the shared authority to implement them.

Indirect Leader. The indirect leader has done a great job with team recruiting and team development. This is obvious, because he can disengage with the team for periods of time and the team will continue to function. Each team member takes ownership for the team's work. They set goals, gather resources, and solve problems, all without the assistance of the indirect leader. The upside of the indirectly led team is that it's a great life experience. The downside is that it's very rare. It only takes one person to disrupt this team. A strong commonality among indirectly led teams is the ability of the team leader to select and develop his team.

Notice in the A-D-I Leadership Approach chart (see Exhibit 17. 1.) how the shifting of authority or communication moves a leader from one style to another.

There are two takeaways from the A-D-I Leadership Approach:

1. *Natural style*. It appears to me that most people have a natural bent in one of these three leadership-style directions. That bent is often displayed in their approach to parenting. If their twenty-one-year-old is told to be in at 10:30 p.m., with no exceptions, they may be leaning toward the autocratic style. If they discuss the advantages and disadvantages of playing in the middle of the interstate with their four-year-old so he can make the right decision, then they may be leaning toward the indirect style. When you're fatigued, stressed, or sleep-deprived, you will find yourself retreating to your default style.

2. *Adaptive style*. Even though you may have a prominent natural style, it's essential that you adapt your style to the individual and the circumstance.

How does the adaptive leader know when to be autocratic, democratic, or indirect? He does so by assessing the circumstance, the individual, the benefits, and the downsides (see Exhibit 17. 2.).

Exhibit 17. 2.				
Preferred Style	**Circumstance**	**Individual**	**Benefits**	**Downsides**
Autocratic	Crises, compliance, legal, safety, leader has the knowledge and expertise, quick decision required	Inexperienced, unfocused, undisciplined, undeveloped skills	Quick decisions, clear chain-of-command, leverages the abilities of strong leaders, consistency, short-term efficiency, time- and cost-effective	Lower team morale, less team input, loss of creativity and ownership, can lead to resentment, less flexible environment
Democratic	Creativity required, buy-in needed, strategy-development, organizational change, team members have greater expertise and knowledge	Engaged, teachable, creative, responsible	Higher team morale, team members feel valued, greater flow of creativity and ideas, encourages flexibility and commitment	Time consuming, creates internal friction, fosters procrastination
Indirect	Long-term projects, high-level projects	High skill set and knowledge base, responsible, committed, team player, problem solver	Leadership development, high level of achievement, ownership of outcome, fuller use of individual expertise and talents	Takes one uncooperative member to disrupt team, feeling neglected by the boss, lack of direction

Team-Building Approach for Teams

So, you have now identified your natural leadership style and you know how to modify that style in response to the circumstance and the individual. But how do you get your team on board and sailing in the same direction?

One conventional method is for management to design a list of team values. Under certain circumstances this can be a useful approach. It helps the team focus on the leadership's expectations for team behavior. However, it has a serious downside.

Both *rules* and *values* are mechanisms that are intended to affect human behavior. Rules, by their very nature, are designed and enforced by someone other than those for whom the rules are designed. Values, on the other hand, are only embraced and enforced by the individual to whom the value applies. No one can tell you what your values are. Only you can. Therefore, when senior leaders create a list of values, they are applying a rules-mentality to values. Good intentions with anemic results. Consider the following **Rules - Values Comparison Analysis** (see Exhibit 17. 3.).

Exhibit 17. 3. RULES - VALUES COMPARISON ANALYSIS	
RULES (laws, regulations, policies, etc.)	**VALUES** (integrity, honesty, patience, etc.)
Negative	Positive
Situation-specific	Universal
Externally designed	Internally designed
Externally enforced	Internally enforced
Downsides	No downsides

- *Negative.* Rules tend to be negative when influencing human behavior. Rules are the fences of human behavior—*don't step over there*. There are ten rules that have been around for a few millennia now, and eight of the ten are written in the negative. *Don't go there!* Values, on the other hand, tend to be positive in nature.
- *Situation-specific.* Rules usually come into existence when a problem, or potential problem, has been discovered. Think Congress. They observe something that is broken and then create a law to fix it. Values, on the other hand, are universal in nature. They apply everywhere, at all times, and in all situations.

- *Externally designed.* Most of the rules under which we live are designed by others. We have family rules designed by parents, workplace policies designed by senior management, school guidelines designed by administrators, safety regulations designed by government agencies, etc. Values, on the other hand, are designed by those who will be living those values.

- *Externally enforced.* Not only are rules designed by external entities, they are enforced by external entities. If we violate a rule, then we will answer to an external enforcer: a parent, a boss, a teacher, a policeman, etc. Values, on the other hand, are not only designed by participants but they are enforced by participants. Participants will determine if there will be a penalty, and if so, what that penalty will be.

- *Downsides.* This is one contrast that is often unobserved. Rules are much more limiting in their function than values because they often have a downside. Think about it. Rules come into existence to address a problem, and at times, the rule itself will come back and haunt us in the very area it was designed to solve. Here's an example.

A small city was working hard to revitalize its inner city. City officials heard that a bank was considering the possibility of constructing a new branch on the edge of town. They developed a plan to coax the bank executives into building their new branch in the inner city instead. They located an empty lot adjacent to a city parking garage and offered the bank executives free use of the city garage for their employees and customers if they built on the empty lot. The bank executives agreed, seeing the potential of building and retaining a customer base with the free-parking offer. The bank executives developed the policy of stamping parking tickets for those who made transactions in the branch to leverage the free parking into creating a larger customer base. It worked great.

However, shortly after the new branch opened, a prominent customer was invited by a VP to come to the branch to consider an investment opportunity. The customer listened to the offer but eventually declined it. On his way out, he stopped at the front desk and asked the customer service representative to stamp his parking ticket. She indicated that she would be delighted to and asked if he had made a transaction. He replied that he had not, but that he was called into the branch by a VP of the bank. With her best customer service smile and empathetic approach, she repeated her desire to stamp his ticket, but that the bank policy required a transaction. Although the bank representative continued to display a great customer service attitude, she tenaciously adhered to the policy. The prominent customer grew more and more agitated. Eventually he thought, *You want a transaction? I'll give you a transaction*, whereby he withdrew his money from the bank.

What was the purpose of the policy in the first place? To increase the customer base. What did the policy eventually do? Decreased the customer base. Rules, by their very nature, often carry a nuanced downside that can come back to haunt us. Values, on the other hand, have no downsides.

Designing Your Team Covenant

Here is your four-step approach to developing a team covenant.

1. Team Covenant: ***Teach it.***

    If you, as a team leader, can't effectively implement values within the team by using a rules-applied approach, what can you do? The following approach may seem radical, but give it a try. It hasn't failed me yet.

    Work with your team to develop a Team Covenant. Start with an instruction session on what a covenant is and why it works.

    Unfortunately, in recent years the word *covenant* has been relegated almost exclusively to the dusty shelves of religion. That is unfortunate; it has not always been that way. For centuries, the word *covenant* was found in common language. Today the word has become almost obsolete outside of the walls of the church. The reason? It has been replaced by the word *contract*. Start by teaching your team the difference between the two words. The following table (see Exhibit 17. 4.) offers a breakdown that might help.

Exhibit 17. 4. CONTRACT - COVENANT COMPARISON ANALYSIS		
	CONTRACT	**COVENANT**
Platform	Built on suspicion	Built on trust
Enforcement	Third-party enforcement	Internal enforcement
Failure	Failure negates contract	Failure does *not* negate covenant

Let's look more closely at the key differences.

- *Platform.* A contract is built on the platform of suspicion. Because the participants distrust each other, they draw up a contract to protect themselves. If I buy your house on a contract-for-deed, we will obviously draw up a contract. This contract exists because you want to make certain that you get your money by the agreed-upon dates, and I want to make certain that you won't arbitrarily take your house back. We have some mutual suspicion about each other. A covenant, on the other hand, is built completely on trust, so no contract is needed.

- *Enforcement.* A contract is enforced by a third party. If one of the contract's participants feels that the other participant has not upheld their end of the contract, then a third party comes into play. That third party will most likely be the judicial system. A covenant, on the other hand, has no third-party enforcement. It's enforced entirely by the participants.

- *Failure.* When a participant fails to uphold their end of the contract, then the consequences for failure are administered by the third party and the contract is often negated. A covenant, on the other hand, will not be voided by failure. If another participant fails to uphold their end of the covenant, the covenant is not voided for me because my commitment to the covenant was not predicated on anyone else's commitment. My commitment is based solely on the credibility of *my* word, not theirs. (You may be starting to see why the word *covenant* has fallen on hard times in our contemporary culture.)

2. Team Covenant: **Design it**.

   After your team has a thorough grasp of the covenant concept, it's time for them to design it. It's my recommendation that they do this independent of the supervisor or manager. You want them to own this. You don't want them to design it because their team leader made them.

   Here is a tip. Most of us think in the rules-mentality when it comes to changing human behavior. It must be the parent in us. A good way to encourage them to identify the values that will be most relevant to them as a team is to first identify the situations and circumstances that cause teams to fail. After they have done this, identify the specific value that would have prevented the circumstance. For example, it's not uncommon for a team member to speak critically of another team member behind their back. This can create resentment and division. A good value that can prevent that is "verbal credibility"—I will speak *about* people in the same way I speak *to* people.

3. Team Covenant: **Sign it**.
    It's one thing to verbally agree to a covenant; it's an entirely different matter to publicly display a team covenant that exhibits the signatures of the team members. This will encourage ownership and follow-through.

4. Team Covenant: **Revisit it**.
    The heavy lifting is in the design of the original team covenant, but the lifting is not over. When the team designs the covenant, designate a date when the team will come back and revisit and potentially modify it. This accomplishes a couple of things. First, it conveys to the team that this is a living document rather than just a cute wall poster. Second, now that they have a feel for how a team covenant works, they will be able to identify other values that would be applicable.

Team goals determine *where* we want to go while a team covenant determines *how* we will conduct ourselves in the process. Many a team has failed to achieve their goals, not because the goals were not well established, or because the team lacked motivation, but because the team had not determined their collective values beforehand.

One final tip—it's probably best to ask a third-party facilitator to work with your team to design the team covenant, especially the first time. Typically, a team has one shot at designing their covenant, and you certainly want them to do it right the first time!

Summary—Here are the building blocks and best practices that will prepare you for tomorrow's leadership challenges.

- Take a candid assessment of your team. Are they dragging Harry? If so, develop a strategy to get the shovel out and bury Harry.
- Review the A-D-I Leadership Approach (see Exhibit 17. 1.). Identify the style that would serve your team the most if you used it more frequently.
- Use a Learning Burst to teach your team the Rules-Values Comparison (see Exhibit 17. 2.).
- Consider developing a Team Covenant. Think it through carefully before you launch. Ask yourself whether it is best for your team if you lead the initiative or if you had an external facilitator lead it. You may only have one shot.

CHAPTER 18

Political Savvy: It Is Not What You Think

Learn how to engage politically without feeling the need to shower afterward.

One of the penalties for refusing to participate in politics
is that you end up being governed by your inferiors.
—PLATO

Workplace politics—this is a tough one. I have the privilege of teaching a workshop at the Federal Executive Institute on political savvy, and I can't remember the last time I was met with an eager class ready to soak in the splendor of workplace politics. Most sane people think "Yuck!" and I get it. However, most of the same people recognize that those who are involved in politics seem to have an advantage when it comes to favorable decisions, which are often centered around resource allocations.

The question arises: *Can a person develop ethical political savvy?* It may sound like an oxymoron, but the answer is a firm *yes*. And the sooner, the better.

I recall a Senior Executive Service (SES) observer who was nearing retirement who approached me after one of the political savvy workshops, and she told me that her big regret was that she had not taken the class thirty years earlier. Her career path, she went on to say, would have had a much different trajectory. Don't let that be said of you.

First, let me allay any ethical concerns that you may have. I will not ask you, nor expect you, to cross the ethical line. Once you do, you are now owned by someone else. Anyone who has knowledge of your unethical action, can leverage that knowledge against you, either overtly or covertly. Not a good place to be. The reason so many of us, myself included, have such a sour view of workplace politics is because they are often conducted by those with elastic ethics. Usually their elastic ethics bend in directions that only benefit them. Think credit thieves, blame-dispensers, and back-stabbers. However, there is a politically savvy path forward that rests between the ethical lines. That is where we are going in this chapter.

Remember when you first stepped into the work arena, believing that if you took ownership for your work, solved problems, avoided trouble, and worked hard, you would be appreciated, recognized, and promoted? How is that working for you? Simultaneously, I suspect that you could come up with the name of a colleague or two who did none of those things and yet were appreciated, recognized, and promoted? Am I right? These two common scenarios have jaded us into withdrawing from politics altogether, or they have caused us to abandon our ethical standards and join the political battles. However, there is a third alternative.

There are three common views of political savvy.

1. *Pollyanna: rose-colored glasses.* This leader looks at the work environment and sees a meritocracy. They want to believe that there is a direct correlation between effort and success, between achievement and recognition, and between personal success and career advancement.
2. *Kill Bill: cynical glasses.* Kill or be killed. This leader looks at the work environment as a Colosseum, and employees are the gladiators. They feel that they have been forced into an arena where they have no option but to survive—and eventually thrive—by going after each other.
3. *Ethical political-savvy: realistic glasses.* This leader has their rose-colored glasses off but refuses to put on their cynical glasses. They are teachable, but not gullible. They develop networking strategies, informal communication venues, negotiating skills, and compromising techniques—all within the ethical lines.

PEER-LEADER QUOTE

Tomorrow's leader is one who thoughtfully and respectfully questions the status quo, uses sincere curiosity to spark the imagination of others and embraces a mindful practice daily to foster meaningful relationships."

JANET WHITE
Retired
Office of Personnel Management

Political Savvy—Why do I need it?

Still not convinced you need to develop your political savvy? Consider the following.

Passive failure is in your future if you do not develop your political savvy. Every organization has a political environment. If you are looking for a politics-free workplace, you have a long search before you.

Think of the most basic and common organizational structure: the family. Are politics involved there? Do kids have political savvy? Of course; that is the only way they make them. Kids will go to one decision-maker in the organization as opposed to another decision-maker—whichever one will give them the most favorable response. Kids have been known to be persistent in the face of "no." Kids have been known to negotiate for a more favorable resource allocation: "I promise I will clean my room and mow the lawn if you loan me twenty dollars." Kids have even been known to go outside of the decision-making process to make an appeal with someone who can influence the internal decision-maker. Think grandparents!

Here's the deal. If you choose not to develop your political savvy in a political environment, then you're setting yourself up for passive failure. You will become a sitting duck for those who have developed their political savvy. Your team may get frustrated with you when they see the favored projects, the increased resources, and the recognition flowing to other teams that have a politically savvy leader.

1. *Surprising success is in your future if you do develop your political savvy.* If you develop your political savvy, then you are about to discover success in surprising arenas. There's a rumor that not all decisions are made linearly in the

org chart. Leaders frequently make decisions taking the political component into consideration.

It was September 17, 1978, when President Jimmy Carter, Israeli Prime Minister Menachem Begin, and Egyptian President Anwar Sadat wrapped up their thirteen-day attempt at drafting a peace accord. Carter indicated in his book *Keeping Faith*[1] that it had been a tumultuous and disappointing time.[38] Carter blended his keen intellect with his southern peanut-farmer charm in an attempt to lead the two antagonists to a peaceful outcome, but to no avail. His thirteen-day attempt at wielding his high-level negotiating skills along with his formal powers of persuasion had now met with bitter disappointment. The sole sticking point was Begin's refusal to sign a letter that had been drafted about Jerusalem.

Carter knew of Begin's love for his grandkids, so he prepared a photograph of the three leaders for each grandchild, along with their individual names on each one. Carter wrote of Begin, "His lips trembled, and tears welled up in his eyes. He told me a little about each child....We were both emotional as we talked quietly for a few minutes about grandchildren and about war....He said, 'I will accept the letter you have drafted on Jerusalem.'" The Camp David Accords were finally agreed upon, leading to the Egypt-Israel Peace Accord, which remains intact to this day. The reason? It was not because of his intellect, high-level negotiating skills, or formal powers of persuasion, but because Carter reached the Prime Minister's heart through his love for his grandchildren.

Why should you develop your political savvy? Success will find you in the most surprising ways and times.

Political Savvy—What Is It?

There are four ways to view any organization. Understanding these four views—or *frames*, as Lee G. Boleman and Terrence E. Deal[2] call them—will provide the context for developing your political savvy.[39] Each leader has an inclination toward subconsciously embracing one of these frames. In fact, you can take an assessment that reveals your dominant frame and your least dominant frame. Try this: Think of your specific organization as we walk through these four frames. How do you see it?

1. *Structural Frame.* When you think of your organization, the ABC Corporation or the Department of the Exterior, you see an organizational chart, divisions,

departments, positions, properties, processes, etc. This is the most common view. When there is a problem, you look at that problem through the *structural* lens and solve the problem accordingly. The solution may involve reorganization, process modification, new or divided departments, new assignments, new positions, etc. *If we just had the right structure in place, no one could stop us.*

2. *Human Resources Frame.* When you think of your organization, you see the power of people. Specific names come to mind. When there is a problem, you look at that problem through the *HR* lens and solve the problem accordingly. The solution may involve hiring the right people, promoting the right people, terminating the right people, training the right people, building the right teams, solving conflicts, and building morale. It's not so much a question of having the right positions; it's a question of having the right people in those positions. *If we just had the right people in the right positions, no one could stop us.*

3. *Symbolic Frame.* When you think of your organization, you see the power of symbolism. If you work for the Department of Defense then you think of the Battle of Iwo Jima, the Normandy invasion, the uniforms, the flag, the medals, the great generals who led our brave troops, and the Medal of Honor recipients. When there is a problem, you look at that problem through the *symbolic* lens and solve the problem accordingly. The solution may involve refreshing the tie between the individual and the greater whole, the organization. *If we just had the right commitment to the organization, no one could stop us.*

4. *Political Frame.* When you think of your organization, you see it consisting of living entities rather than structure, people, or symbolism. You believe your organization consists of stakeholder groups consisting of one or more people competing for favorable decisions and sparse resources. When there is a problem, you look at that problem through the *political* lens and solve the problem accordingly. The solution may involve informal negotiations, developing networks and allies, collaborating with non-traditional partners, and developing strategic relationships. *If we just had the right influence with the relevant entities, no one could stop us.*

So, what's your dominant frame? What's your least dominant frame? Your effectiveness, not to mention your career, will take on new influence if you can learn to view your organization through each one of these frames. Try this: Examine a daunting workplace challenge through each of these frames separately. Take one frame at a time and brainstorm solutions solely from that frame. Then repeat the process using the other frames one at a time.

Political Savvy—How Do I Do It?

How do you start developing your political-savvy skills? Let me suggest three areas to get you going.

1. *Develop your political perspective.* If you see political savvy as the property of those who break the rules, of narcissists, of the ethically challenged, and of the social manipulators, you will struggle with your political savvy development. You need to come to peace with the realization that political savvy will always be needed, and it can be wielded by good people, doing good things, with good intentions, and with good outcomes. When you find yourself there, you are ready to start.

2. *Develop your informal political skillsets.* There are many skills that may not be on your Personal Development Plan (PDP) because they don't directly advance your vocational aspirations. It is time to reconsider and add some of those neglected skills. Revise your PDP to include political savvy development. Just to clarify, I am talking about informal skills. Skills that can be used one-on-one. Start with informal negotiation skills. Discover the power of informal negotiations and learn how to utilize it. Add personal persuasion skills to your negotiation skills. Robert B. Cialdini, Ph.D., in his best seller *The Psychology of Persuasion,*[3] lays out six scientific shortcuts to influence others through persuasion.[40] They are *Reciprocity*—people repay in kind; *Scarcity*— people value what's scarce; *Authority*—people defer to experts who provide shortcuts to decisions requiring specialized information; *Consistency*—people fulfill written, public, and voluntary commitments; *Liking*— people like those who like them; and *Consensus*—people follow the lead of similar others. They are worth exploring and adding to your political-savvy toolbox. The third skillset you need to develop is informal conflict management. I didn't say resolution, but management. The HR frame looks at conflict as counterproductive, but the political frame looks at conflict as the potential for breakthroughs with intractable problems, nudging people out of

entrenched views, forming new alliances, and for analyzing the tethers to significance.

3. *Develop your political partnerships (collaborating).* If you listen carefully, you can hear the crumbling of silos across organizations. The old tribal mentality, along with the protection of its territory, is beginning to give way to collaborative partnerships. We are seeing leaders within an organization developing collaborative partnerships with entities that have long been considered opponents. We see leaders collaborating with others from different silos like those in the public, private, academic, NGO, and civic sectors. We see secure leaders exploring collaborative partnerships with long standing competitors; a "collaboratiton" if you will. When developing your collaborative partnerships, consider the fact that there are four levels of cooperation (see Exhibit 18.1.).

Exhibit 18. 1. Collaboration Levels	
Information	Sharing of data, solutions, management practices, trends.
Execution	Sharing of actions and projects.
Possessions	Sharing of budgets and resources.
Associations	Sharing of organization, accountability, and outcomes.

You can simply collaborate with *information* by exchanging mutually beneficial data, solutions, management practices, trends, etc. You can also ratchet up the collaboration by adding *execution* to the effort. Here you engage with mutual actions. You join forces with certain projects. You can also take it to the next level by adding *possessions*. This is where you start sharing some resources and budgets. Finally, you can collaborate with a mutual *association*. Here is where your mutual confidence has grown to the point where sharing of *information, execution,* and *possessions* has led to the birth of a formal *association*.

The political frame is the least represented of the four frames, and by a substantial margin. For most of us, it's the most difficult frame to use. That's the bad news. The good news is that the opportunities are immense. If you ethically cultivate your political savvy, your career path will take a whole new trajectory and your workplace impact will surge.

Summary—Here are the building blocks and best practices that will prepare you for tomorrow's leadership challenges.

- Ask yourself if you are prepared to engage in ethical politics. If not, explore the reasons for your reluctance and set out a strategy to overcome them.
- Ask yourself if you see the value of elevating your political-savvy skills. Remember, awareness of need is one of the greatest learning incentives.
- Develop your informal negotiation skills.
- Explore Robert B. Cialdini's six scientific shortcuts to effective persuasion.
- Identify some potential political partnerships for collaboration. Determine what level is best for each partnership. Make it happen!

CHAPTER 19

Time Management, and Other Myths

> The trouble with being in a rat race
> is that even if you win the race,
> you are still a rat.
> —LILY TOMLIN

We have been duped!

Once those fancy new computers come out, you will be looking at a five-hour workday and a four-day work week. Technology will enable you to get so much more done in a shorter period, enabling you to enjoy larger amounts of free time. Or so we were told years ago when we were on the cusp of the technological age. How is that working for you? Are you enjoying all that extra free time?

Few of us are—because just the opposite has happened. Technological advances have put more work on our plates and have stolen more of our free time. I hope that you have discovered by now that you alone are the one who will determine your time usage. If you depend on others to determine your free time, then you will become a slave to others. Think about it: All we are asked to do as leaders today is to get more done, with fewer resources, and to get it done faster.

However, there is some encouraging generational data on this front. Baby boomers chose *work over life*. Hang a dollar bill in front of a boomer and we'll be working Saturdays. Speak to any boomer about their life and you will often hear statements of regret about not spending more time with the kids, about not taking the allotted vacation time, about working too much overtime, about not travelling when they had their health, etc. We chose *work over life*.

Along came Gen Xers. After observing the lives of their parents, they said, "I don't think so. Not going to do it." They chose a *work-life balance*. Work and career are important, but not all-important.

Then came the millennials and they took it to the next step—*life over work*. They view work as ancillary to life. They aren't looking for balance, they're looking for life experiences, in the hopes that work may assist them in that pursuit. Some even talk of mid-life retirement, where they take off work for a few years to travel or maybe go back to school. They are less inclined to self-define by what they do, or by the career they have chosen. Granted, some millennials have taken this too far, but regretfully, so did many boomers with their view of life and work.

Regardless of the generational views, time management must start with the larger picture, and that is: *Time is the measurement of the passing of your life*. Therefore, when you allow others to determine what you do with your time, you're letting others determine what you are going to do with your life.

The Great Myth

You can manage your time. That's it. That's the myth.

No one manages their time because time is unmanageable. It is a fixed resource of which everyone has an equal allocation. It doesn't matter whether you're in the White House, the school house, the jail house, the doghouse, or your house. We all have the same 24/7 allocation. There is nothing there to manage. What we really mean when we use the phrase "time management," is "self-management." It's managing what I do with the limited resource of time.

Self-management within the context of time is tough...and deceptive. During my years as a counselor, I observed that highly ambitious people who were stressed out felt that they had little control of their time. They saw themselves as part of the rat race, from which there was no exit. It's not that the exits weren't there. The exits were there, but they were very unattractive. The exit signs were labeled with "declined promotion"; "fewer or older vehicles"; "smaller house"; "state school for kids"; "shorter or fewer vacations"; and "less prestige." If you're serious about managing time, chew on this question. Are you *driven* or are you *led*? If you don't feel that you can choose your exits, then you're being driven. If you can choose your exits, then you're being led. You're being led by your values and priorities. If you feel that you're in the rat race, and you're looking for a time-efficiency tip or technique to liberate you, then you are deceiving yourself. Exiting the rat race is not a question of finding the right processes, it's a question of following your values-driven priorities.

Our values flow through two channels—how we invest our possessions and how we invest our time. If you monitored my expenditures from my bank accounts and you monitored my schedule, you could tell me what my values are. If those channels display values that are other than the values I say I admire and embrace, then I will live a life with serious dissonance. Think *driven*, think stress.

The Eisenhower Decision Model

You think you have it bad with the time-pressures you face. Just consider the pressure that General Dwight D. Eisenhower was under as commander of the Allied Forces early in the summer of 1944. The Allied forces were about to embark on the largest sea invasion in history. The outcome was less than clear. Not only did the fortunes of World War II fall on his shoulders; so did the young lives of thousands of soldiers, sailors, and aviators. The demands for his time and energy must have felt other-worldly. So how did this general and soon-to-be president decide how best to schedule his time? How was he able to stay centered and yet accomplish all that needed to be accomplished?

The answer didn't reside in utilizing certain techniques and tips. It didn't even reside in the development of certain tried-and-true time-management skills. Instead, the solution was found in a principle. A principle that helped him stay tethered to significance throughout the incessant pressures of time-demand. He clearly defined that principle by drawing a contrast between two words that we all too frequently conflate.

In 1954 President Dwight D. Eisenhower laid out his tethered-to-significance approach to time at Northwestern University in Evanston, Illinois, during the Second

Assembly of the World Council of Churches, by quoting a former, unnamed president. "I have two kinds of problems, the urgent and the important. The urgent are not *important*, and the important are never *urgent*."[1] Urgency has to do with time, but importance has to do with value. You may face something that is both urgent and important, but one does not make the other true.

Your life wasn't given to you to practice with. If you don't make values-based choices, then welcome to the rat race. Your time-decisions will be made by urgency and you will feel driven. However, if you tether yourself to significance and you make the hard decisions based on your values, then you will feel more in control of your time. That means more control of your life.

Process Tips

Even though process tips and techniques will not liberate you from the rat race, they still have practical value on a day-to-day basis. Here are twenty tips and techniques that I would recommend you consider as tomorrow's leader; they may help you self-manage toward greater efficiency.

1. *Develop values-vetting for tasks.* Is this *important* or is it *urgent*?
2. *Box your time.* Your productivity per hour increases when you predetermine your time constraints.
3. *Defragment your schedule and prepare work for time gaps.* Look for unproductive moments like travel time, waiting times, water-cooler times, online time, etc., and have tasks ready to complete during those gaps.
4. *Go home on time.* If you take the position that you will go home when your work is done, as opposed to a predetermined time, then your productivity per hour decreases.
5. *Reclaim the 21-minute day.* If you convert twenty-one unproductive minutes into productive minutes every day, then you will give yourself a full eight-hour additional day every month.
6. *Improve your phone skills.* Learn to economize your phone calls through the use of surgical questions and direct conversation.
7. *Call social butterflies after hours so you can leave a voice mail.* Enough said.
8. *Group your phone calls.* When you dedicate a window of time for your phone calls, instead of interspersing them throughout the day, you will increase your time efficiency. Interruptions not only steal the actual time invested in the

interruption; they steal time after the interruption. It takes time to reengage with our previous task, especially if deep thought or creativity is involved.

9. *Make calls in scheduling gaps.* Phone calls are great candidates for contributing to the 21-minute rule.

10. *Use polite, but direct, conversation stoppers.* Be prepared with phrases that you can use in any conversation that will politely free you from that conversation.

11. *Keep emails to one monitor.* Everyone loves short and concise emails. Challenge yourself to say what is needed in the least amount of space.

12. *BLUF.* "Bottom line up front." Write your email with the bottom line at the top. Better yet, put it in the subject line.

13. *Use numbered lists in emails.* People consume online information in the form of lists. We tend to think linearly, so write linearly. Instead of burying the information in a paragraph, write it in a list. Use numbers instead of bullet points to enable ease of referencing.

14. *Separate your to-do list from your can-do list.* Keep your to-do list clean. Only include the things that you *must* complete. Make a second list for those things you can do if you have enough time.

15. *Hold stand-up meetings.* If your meetings are dragging out due to a proneness on the participant's part to wander, then try stand-up meetings. People are more inclined to stay on track and focused when standing than when sitting.

16. *Use the "rip-n-read" approach to magazines.* You know how this one works. You have that shiny new magazine sitting on your desk. You think, "When I get the time, I will read it." Before you realize it, the next month's edition has come, and last month's edition remains unread. Try this instead: The day the magazine shows up, peruse the contents and rip out the article or articles that catch your interest; then throw the rest of the shiny new magazine away. Ironically, you may find yourself actually reading more magazines when you throw them away on the first day.

17. *Use minutes instead of hours for scheduling meetings and phone calls.* If you find people wasting your time by showing up late for meetings, or not being available for the scheduled phone call because another appointment they had ran late, try this. Avoid scheduling your meetings and phone calls at the top or bottom of the hour. In American culture, 10:00 a.m. means "ten-ish." Schedule your meetings and phone calls at 9:10 or 2:40. Anytime you break a time measurement down to the next smaller unit, you increase the perception of importance.

18. *Learn to say "no."* You may have to practice this in the mirror in the mornings, but give it a try. Learn how and when to say "no."

19. *Assertively handle social butterflies.* It is generally considered rude to look at the time on your watch or phone when in a conversation with a social butterfly. This is true, but there is a way that you can do this without being perceived as rude. Look at the time when *you* are talking as opposed to when *they* are talking. If you look at the time when you are talking, then you are cutting yourself off, not them.

20. *Use the four-D vetting system.* As a supervisor, should I dump it, delegate it, delay it, or do it?

Summary—Here are the building blocks and best practices that will prepare you for tomorrow's leadership challenges.

- Schedule an appointment with yourself in a remote location, with the intent of analyzing your usage of time using one question—Am I being driven, or am I being led? Deeply ponder whether your time is being primarily invested by external circumstances, or whether your time investments accurately reflect your priorities and values.

- Select three self-management ideas from the list of twenty Process Tips and devise a plan to integrate them into your routine.

CHAPTER 20

What Is...What Is to Be

Process and purpose!

> Life must be understood backward.
> But it must be lived forward.
> —Søren Kierkegaard

Our caramel macchiatos are almost gone, and it's time to part paths. But before you go, give me one last shot at putting this all together.

How old are you?

Age is an odd measurement. When a person dies, we stop celebrating their birthday. That means when we do celebrate birthdays, we are essentially celebrating the fact that they didn't die in the last year. Although it's impossible, age should be measured from the present until death, rather than from birth to the present. Birthdays are really deceitful indicators of how old we are. If a millennial gets terminal cancer and is given six months to live, they are much "older" than a healthy boomer.

John Lennon told us in his final album, "Life is what happens to you while you're busy making other plans."[1] For many of us, a life of meaning will take place at some foggy point in the future. Meanwhile, we surf through life on the waves of responsibilities. There is another way.

Stephen Covey told us that all good leaders begin with the end in mind. That is true. But the leader who is tethered to significance applies that first to life, and secondly to leadership.

So, what does the end look like? It's unfortunate that our culture separates people from death. Many of us have never spent time with someone who is near death. It's unfortunate, because these loved ones who are near death often have complete candor, honesty, and lucidity. There's no longer a need on their part to impress, deceive, or pretend.

Bonnie Ware is a palliative nurse who cares for those who have entered the final twelve weeks of their lives. She has fastidiously monitored and recorded the deathbed regrets of hundreds of patients over the course of many years. These patients were near death—not quite there, but very near.

From her recordings came a book titled *The Top Five Regrets of the Dying.*[2] Here are some of the most common sentiments she heard:

I wish I'd had the courage to live a life true to myself, not the life others expected of me.

I wish I hadn't worked so hard.

I wish I'd had the courage to express my feelings.

I wish I had stayed in touch with my friends.

I wish that I had let myself be happier.

There it is. There's the majority vote of the dead when it comes to beginning with the end in mind.

People who encounter a *near-death experience*, only to survive, often speak of a revitalized sense of life's value. They speak of savoring afresh the pleasure of daily life, and more importantly, they make different life choices based on that fresh view of time. All too many of us are obliviously trapped in a numbing *near-life experience* where we know of time's fleeting value, but we still don't make better decisions based on that knowledge. We are near life—not quite there, but very near.

So, how do we get there? Nancy Duarte is a student of storytelling. She observed that all great stories involve two components: "What is," and "What is to be."[3] A picture of the present, followed by a clear picture of what will be. As a leader for tomorrow, realize that your story does not have to keep being "What is." You can take active steps toward "What is to be."

However, your journey to "What is to be" is fraught with external challenges.

Culture. Culture will continue its attempt to seduce you with scintillating processes. Do you remember the root word for technology? *Technique*—and *technique* describes a process. It helps us with the *how* of life, but not the *why* of life. Technology has penetrated all aspects of life with glimmering splendor, and it's only beginning. The leaders of tomorrow must be current with available technology—the latest processes.

However, these leaders must not allow these processes to masquerade as contributors to *purpose*. Allowing them to do so will fray your tethers. "Those who have a 'why' to live, can bear with almost any 'how.'"[4]

Criticism. If you tether yourself to significance, you will be swimming upstream. You will face brutal criticism. Your decision-making will be met with skepticism, and at times, outright hostility.

If I held up a one-hundred-dollar bill in front of a group of people and asked them, "How many of you would like to have this bill?", how many would raise their hand? Certainly, a strong majority; like, everyone! If I took that same one-hundred-dollar bill and crushed it into a tiny little ball and then repeated the question, the same number of people would still want it even though I crushed it. And if I took that same crumpled ball of a bill and dropped it on the dirty floor, crushed it under my dirty shoe, and then asked, "Now how many want this bill?", everyone would still want it. Why? Because its intrinsic value never changes.

The day will come, if it hasn't already, when someone will say something to you or about you that will absolutely crush you. Tears may come, sleep may escape you, but it doesn't change your intrinsic value one bit. The day may come when you give your ethical all as a leader who is tethered to significance, and after having done so, you are not recognized for your achievement—you are passed over for that promotion that you so richly deserve. You feel totally stepped on after having given your ethical all. But remember, it doesn't change your intrinsic value one bit.

All good leaders begin with the end in mind…and if you waded through these twenty chapters, then you are at least an aspiring good leader. It's been a while since you dipped your toe into the Preface of this book and it was there that I laid out my solitary ambition—"that you—and those you influence—are better by the time you finish reading the last chapter. It is my hope that you will become smarter, more courageous, more determined, more focused, more empathetic, more effective, more ambitious, more content, and more tethered to significance. Build your tethers, and the tethers of those you lead, by approaching influence from the inside out.

I would love to hear about your *what is to be*!

Michael A. Hovda
mhovda@isnsideoutleadership.com

Peer-Leadership Quotations

Some hand-selected leaders from a variety of management levels and from a variety of work environments were asked to contribute their thoughts regarding the future needs of tomorrow's leader. These individuals are numbered among the author's friends, colleagues, and clients, and their insights are greatly appreciated.

Each leader responded to the statement, **"Tomorrow's leader is one who ______________."** (Choose one of the following words to help you complete the statement: *is, never, always, thinks, considers, acts,* etc.)

Marinate in their insights, which have been forged on the front lines of leadership. They are your peers.

1. Tomorrow's leader is one who empathetically leads/advises and is not afraid to show humility towards subordinates at the appropriate times.

    Danny W. White, CIV, DAF
    Chief, Education Operations Branch
    Air Force Special Operations Command
    A1KE

2. Tomorrow's leader is one who realizes the potential in people and cultivates their potential to produce the best possible results.

    Tomorrow's leader is an agent of change and doesn't allow fear or unintended consequences to get in the way of achieving progress.

    Marie Gayo
    President
    Trident Mortgage Company
    Berkshire Hathaway HomeServices Fox & Roach

3. Leadership is constantly asking oneself the question, "Would I follow me?

    Wilder Smith
    Branch Manager
    TSA Intelligence Planning & Programs Division

4. Tomorrow's leader...
    - promotes bold and thoughtful leadership, accountability, ownership, empowerment, and innovation.
    - values collaboration, mutual respect, and teamwork.
    - is a Servant Leader, ensuring employees are motivated and have what they need to perform their best.
    - is always in improvement mode and continuously learning.
    - recognizes the value of leadership-skills development and mentoring.
    - doesn't need to have a title or position to be a leader; rather, they create or take the opportunities to lead.
    - is never satisfied with the status quo and is willing to put in the work to improve.

Jean T Dumlao, PE, CEM
Director, Public Works
Naval Facilities Engineering Command
Mid-Atlantic

5. Tomorrow's leader understands the bridge between leading change and managing operational excellence.

Jeremy Long
Senior Manager
Sustainable Packaging
Amazon.com

6. Tomorrow's leader is one who delivers outcomes at the speed of life, business, technology, and innovation.

Rob Denson
President
Des Moines Area Community College

7. Tomorrow's leader is one who has the ability to create a sense of stability during times of organizational uncertainty.

R. "Tim" Yoho, DPM
Dean of the College of Podiatric Medicine and Surgery
Des Moines University

8. Tomorrow's leader is one who can harness the power of resilience.

Chris Koroknay
Creative Director
Studio CK

9. Tomorrow's leader is the one who leads with a servant's heart and is willing to let others succeed.

Doug Holloway
VP, Construction
Taylor Morrison

10. Tomorrow's leader is one who cares for those he's leading!

Steve Harthoorn
Founder and Owner
Pella Precast Products, Inc.

11. Tomorrow's leader is one who embraces and inspires innovative solutions.

Lanatta R. Clark, MSN, RN,
Chief Organizational Development
Department of Veterans Affairs

12. Tomorrow's leader is one who considers him- or herself the chief learning officer of the organization.

Ben Dattner
Dattner Consulting

13. Tomorrow's leader must be a plain and simple, humble, and inspirational leader who understands the essentials of industrial democracy and social betterment.

Joe Schumacher
Fire Chief (Ret.)
Arvada, CO

14. Tomorrow's leader is one who knows the right decisions to make and when to make them.

Jonathan Meyer
Youth Pastor
Grace Church
Des Moines, IA

15. Tomorrow's leader is one who puts others first, expects less, and gives more.

Hagen Harker
President
Mid-States Concrete Industries

16. Tomorrow's leader is one who gains wisdom, cares about people, and serves in humility with gratitude.

Mike Broerman
McCoy, Faulkner, and Broerman Law Firm

17. True leadership is empowering those in need with your heart.

Craig M. Powers
AVP
Sr. Engineering Specialist
FM Global

18. Tomorrow's leader is one who can communicate the corporate vision while maintaining daily reality.

David Goos
Substitute Teacher
Newton Community Schools

19. Leadership is the art of Creating the Future.

Fred Lang, PhD
Golden Pines Associates, LLC
Leadership Lessons from Great World Leaders (2017)
American Press Publishers

20. Tomorrow's leader is one who thoughtfully and respectfully questions the status quo, uses sincere curiosity to spark the imagination of others, and embraces a mindful practice daily to foster meaningful relationships.

Janet White
US Office of Personnel Management (Ret.)

21. Tomorrow's leader is one who always remembers: kind mercy wins over harsh judgment every time (James 2:13).

Margaret Ratcliff
President
Midwestone Insurance Services, Inc.

22. Tomorrow's leader is one who leads by example and genuinely cares about the welfare of his followers.

Dan Birkenholz
Birkenholz Realty

23. Tomorrow's leader is one who implements golden nuggets gleaned from others as catalysts for growth.

Kurt Olsen
President
TCS Consulting

24. Tomorrow's leader is a person that people buy into first, before buying into a thought.

Rick Shutts
Regional Manager
Spahn & Rose Lumber Co.

25. Leadership is having vision for a group or organization and the confidence to motivate others toward that goal.

Royal Roland
Roland & Dieleman, CPAs

26. Leadership is one who never squanders an opportunity to teach.

Phil Doak
Owner
Doak Design

27. Tomorrow's leader is one who has integrity and perseverance, who embraces change, and who creates more leaders.

Connie Wimer
Owner
"Business Record"

28. Tomorrow's leader is one who considers differing views and acts based on principles and integrity.

Donald G. Klein
Deputy to the President
National Credit Union Administration

29. Leadership is sharing an idea and inspiring others to reach it.

Hal Pitt
Hal Pitt Seminars
Founder and CEO

30. Don't let the 24/7 connection to your job become your life; remember the combination of you, family, and friends created your success, so always find time to maintain these important relationships.

I close the day with the following question under my desk pad; would the following have been proud of me today? Son, Wife, Parents, God? My response helps me refocus for the next day.

Mark Peiffer
Senior Vice President and Chief Financial Officer
Des Moines University

APPENDIX B

My GPS Action Plan

...and bookmark! Tear this page out and use it as your bookmark.
The specifics of my personal *what is to be* are found below.

My *what is to be* action item.   **Page Number**

1. ____

2. ____

3. ____

4. ____

5. ____

6. ____

7. ____

8. ____

9. ____

10. ____

11. ____

12. ____

13. ____

14. ____

15. ____

16. ____

17. ____

Testimonials

Mike Hovda has worked with Des Moines University over the last couple of years to help us improve our leadership and communication skills. His insights and ability to build rapport with a diverse group of people has been very helpful to me and my leadership team. I am proud to recommend Hovda and Associates, Inc. and InsideOutLeadership.

Terry E. Branstad
President and CEO, Des Moines University
(Longest-serving governor [Iowa] in US history)
US Ambassador to China

I have known Mike Hovda for over four years; we engaged Mike and his company InsideOutLeadership at one of our largest facilities (ThyssenKrupp Budd Canada) in Ontario, Canada, where I was at that time recently named the president and chairman of the board.

Our future was in question with a number of difficult questions facing us as we looked at the road ahead. We were reopening our labor agreement after only signing a new Collective Bargaining Agreement six months earlier; to be successful we needed strategic help in training our management team in providing the proper leadership for our employees.

Mike and InsideOutLeadership provided required training and leadership our team needed to manage the workforce as we went through this transition, I personally developed a great respect for Mike and his methods. I have remained in touch with him over the years and in the future would never hesitate to call upon him to lead an organization through any transitional or improvement process.

Earl E. Kansier
President and Chairman of the Board
ThyssenKrupp Budd Canada

Mike Hovda's seminars are an un-missable feast. He is a "top-drawer" speaker who engages his audience with relevant real-life experiences, stories, and sound solutions, ensuring his audience leaves with a lot more than when they arrived. As a "delighted" customer of his seminars, I can only recommend.

Susan Burn
Siemens Business Services
Performance Management
United Kingdom

Michael Hovda of InsideOutLeadership has been a key contributor to Bookspan's employee development training program for the past five years. Right from the very start, Michael quickly gained credibility with management as well as employees because of his ability to relate to their business needs and his delivery of practical training solutions.

Through our on-site training program, Michael developed and delivered ten to twenty training seminars each year. Each seminar focused on specific training topics that were selected by reviewing employee needs as well as incorporating current strategic business initiatives. Many of the seminars incorporated the use of various assessment tools that provided valuable individual feedback to training participants.

Michael was always willing to customize training from InsideOutLeadership's impressive course catalog, as well as develop new training material to suit a specific need. In addition, Michael delivered and adapted training to various employee levels and groups, hosted in either the corporate headquarters or operating division locations.

Michael's course evaluations speak for themselves, as our employees continue to rate his content and delivery as excellent.

Cheryl A. Cucco
Vice President, Human Resources
Time Warner Company

Michael Hovda of InsideOutLeadership currently conducts numerous training seminars for Bookspan, a partnership of AOL Time Warner and Bertelsmann AG. Bookspan conducts over forty on-site classes for employees each year, and Mike continues to be rated number one by our employees and managers.

As we strive to expand and offer relevant classes for our company, we take a great deal of time in surveying employees and conducting reviews of the classes we offer. I would overwhelmingly recommend Mike for any soft-skill seminar ranging from communications skills to project management skills. He is an excellent creator of new material and recently designed a new class based on management issues we were having. He is highly competitive and a true professional!

Kelly McCarthy
Vice President, Human Resources
BMG Columbia House

I have had the privilege of working with Mike Hovda over the past several years, and without a doubt he is one of the most gifted individuals I have had the pleasure of observing. Whether he is providing group training sessions, department-wide personnel interventions, or one-on-one career counseling, Mike's ability to work with people sets the bar very high. He is well rooted in the needs of the business world and is able to deliver sound, professional advice to those who need direction or for those who simply wish to improve themselves.

After having utilized his services on multiple occasions, several individuals came to me personally and said that he had a strong impact on them, which they believed would help them meet their professional goals. Mike is an individual who values integrity, competency, and proficiency, and he has seamlessly incorporated these values into the training and services he provides.

Because of Mike's keen ability to quickly assess needs, he is capable of providing invaluable services to everyone, regardless of the industry, stage of an individual's career, or work-place needs.

Kiley Mars
HR Director
Des Moines University

Having Mike Hovda from InsideOutLeadership work with our enrollment team has resulted in a tremendously positive transformation. We have gone from a fragmented group, functioning but without synergy, to a much more cohesive, collaborative, and student-centered team. Mike's ability to listen, observe, and appropriately diagnose areas for improvement—and then target those with effective strategies—has put us in a position to move forward much more productively and cooperatively. We are very grateful for Mike's wisdom, leadership, and patience in guiding us through this transformation.

Margaret Gehringer
Director of Enrollment Management
Des Moines University

I have had the pleasure of working with Mike Hovda for over five years, first at Bookspan and now at Bertelsmann Direct North America. I can attest to his knowledge in both management development and training. Mike's training classes get the highest ratings from both managers and employees in addition to helping our company with challenging coaching projects. In today's cost-containment environment, his training continues to add value for our company.

Kelly McCarthy
VP, Human Resources
Bertelsmann Direct North America

What made Mike's presentation about *Managing During Times of Change* so memorable was his ability not only to lead attendees in learning about how to recognize people's fear of change, but also to help them understand the tactics needed to alleviate those fears and increase performance. Mike provided both theory and practice, and I'm able to make use of both with my own team.

Steve Martin
Managing Editor
MacDonald Advertising Services

I spoke to some of my branch directors the day after Hovda and Associates' workshop and they were all excited about having had the opportunity to actually apply the concepts to real-life situations. They were also energized from having had the chance to work in team situations with their peers. I think we'll see multiple specific benefits from this event.

Phil Feldman
VP Home Healthcare
Loving Care Agency, Inc.

Yesterday I met Mike Hovda from InsideOutLeadership at a Print Summit I attended in our area. He presented on the Y generation and how to work with them—what "we" need to understand about them...it was awesome. I learned so much from the presentation, I can't even begin to place a value on the time I spent.

Having several Gen Y–ers on staff, I thought I was getting "too old" to do this anymore, but those thoughts were washed from my mind as I listened with delight as Mike told us how to "manage" these critters—allowing everyone to stay sane, and the business to move to the next generation without totally losing our minds. Mike provided REAL stuff…not just pump-up-the-chest material.

Sandy Andreasen
Business Growth Strategist

To compete effectively in today's market, we knew we had to have outstanding management, leadership, and communication capabilities. To achieve these, we needed not just another vendor, but an educational partner who thoroughly understood our needs and goals. InsideOutLeadership was able to instantly offer a customized program tailored to our training challenges. Mr. Hovda is truly one of the best trainers that I have had the opportunity and pleasure to work with.

Brent Wimsatt
Manager, Human Resources
ThyssenKrupp Budd

Our staff still speaks of Mike's seminar. I hope that we can utilize Mike's services again in the future. I think all we'd have to do is mention his name and our staff would arrive a day early! Mike definitely has a talent for teaching and motivating.

Wendy McMullen
HR Director
Northwest Federal Savings Bank

In all my years of attending trade conferences, I was most compelled by what Mike Hovda shared. His insight to the 24/7 lives of our talent pool really opened my eyes to a completely new way to lead and develop my team. I was encouraged by his direction to return to my office and take immediate action. In fact, my notes are taped to the back of my office door as constant reminders.

Tony Bernados
Classified Multimedia Director
August Chronicle
President of SCAMA

I'm preparing for an interview to fill a vacant position here at Trident. I'm referring back to the *Hiring Skills* workbook Mike Hovda gave us a couple of years ago. I do this every time and I can't tell you how much more prepared I am than I used to be. I really enjoy using the skills and questions that we learned in his course.

Ken Kirkner
Vice President of Operations
Trident Land Transfer Company
Berkshire Hathaway HomeServices Fox & Roach

ThyssenKrupp Budd measured pre- and post-training productivity to determine the impact of Hovda and Associates ten-day supervisor training program for their new supervisors. They discovered an increase in the Press Shop of fourteen strokes per hour, which is an increase of 336 per day! They also found an overall increase in performance on A shift of 4 percent, while C shift enjoyed an 8 percent increase!

Ron Trandell
Area Manager
ThyssenKrupp Budd

Mike Hovda's presentation on *Conflict Management* was rich with useful information and high in inspiration. The attendees were engaged and entertained. Mike is one of the best speakers I have heard.

Gail Sillman
Executive Director
Central Massachusetts Independent Physicians Association (CMIPA)

ACKNOWLEDGMENTS

For my friends, colleagues, and clients who provided the Peer Leaders quotes scattered throughout this book, and that are preserved in appendix A. These crisp quotes from hand-selected leaders, representing all levels of management and diverse work environments, provide keen insights from those who fight leadership battles daily.

This one is more like an apology than an acknowledgment, but for the many who have contributed to my career. You may very well find your unattributed insights in these pages. How does it go? "An original thinker is one who hides his sources well." It is also one who is privileged to have so many contributors that he forgets the sources. Thank you for letting me glom onto your knowledge and wisdom. Nietzsche told us, "A good author possesses not only his own intellect, but also that of his friends."[1]

To my wife, Marilyn, and to my kids—Rachel, Jeremy, Bethany, and Nathanael—who help keep me tethered to significance.

NOTES

Chapter 1

1. Eric Katz (June 18, 2018) "The Federal Agencies Where the Most Employees Are Eligible to Retire," *Government Executive.* https://www.govexec.com/pay-benefits/2018/06/federal-agencies-where-most-employees-are-eligible-retire/149091/?oref=top-story.

2. Serhat Kurt (October 24, 2016) "Kirkpatrick Model: Four Levels of Learning Evaluation," *Educational Technology.* https://educationaltechnology.net/kirkpatrick-model-four-levels-learning-evaluation.

Chapter 3

1. Mark Twain. Cited on: BrainyQuote.com, BrainyMedia Inc., 2019. https://www.brainyquote.com/quotes/mark_twain_100358.

2. Warren Bennis. Cited in: Cecil O. Kemp, Jr., *Wisdom Honor & Hope: The Inner Path to True Greatness* (The Wisdom Company, Inc. 2000), p. 207.

3. Martin Luther King (1968) "I Have a Dream," Speech presented at the March on Washington for Jobs and Freedom, Washington, D.C. http://avalon.law.yale.edu/20th_century/mlk01.asp.

4. WarrenBennis (1997) *Managing People Is Like Herding Cats. Provo, UT: Executive Excellence Publishing,* p. 89.

5. George Orwell. Cited on: BrainyQuote.com, BrainyMedia Inc., 2019. https://www.brainyquote.com/quotes/george_orwell_189106.

6. Niall McCarthy (June 29, 2018) "The Institutions Americans Trust Most and Least In 2018 [Infographic]." https://www.forbes.com/sites/niallmccarthy/2018/06/29/the-institutions-americans-trust-most-and-least-in-2018-infographic/#1ad5ac582fc8.

7. Colin Powell (February 11, 2011) "The Essence of Leadership." https://www.youtube.com/watch?v=ocSw1m30UBI&t=6s.

Chapter 5

1. Skye Gould and Lauren F. Friedman (February 4, 2016) "Something startling is going on with antidepressant use around the world," *Business Insider.* https://www.businessinsider.com/countries-largest-antidepressant-drug-users-2016-2.

2. Daniel Kurt (May 9, 2019) "Are You in the Top One Percent of the World?", *Investopedia.* https://www.investopedia.com/articles/personal-finance/050615/are-you-top-one-percent-world.asp.

3. WorldData. "Average Income Around the World," https://www.worlddata.info/average-income.php.

4. Mark J. Perry (June 5, 2016) "New US homes today are 1,000 square feet larger than in 1973 and living space per person has nearly doubled," *American Enterprise Institute.* http://www.aei.org/publication/new-us-homes-today-are-1000-square-feet-larger-than-in-1973-and-living-space-per-person-has-nearly-doubled.

5. Olivia Heath (October 12, 2017) "This Is the Average Size Home in England and Wales – and how it compares to the EU & USA." https://www.housebeautiful.com/uk/lifestyle/property/news/a2590/average-uk-property-size-comparison.

Chapter 6

1. Gilbert K. Chesterton. Cited on: BrainyQuote.com, *BrainyMedia Inc,* 2019. https://www.brainyquote.com/quotes/gilbert_k_chesterton_161974.

2. Friedrich Nietzsche. Cited on: BrainyQuote.com, *BrainyMedia Inc,* 2019. https://www.brainyquote.com/quotes/friedrich_nietzsche_103819.

Chapter 8

1.   Daniel Kahneman (2011) *Thinking, Fast and Slow.* New York, NY: Farrar, Straus and Giroux.

2.   Jerry B. Harvey (1974) "The Abilene Paradox: The Management of Agreement," *Southeastern Homepages.* http://homepages.se.edu/cvonbergen/files/2013/01/The-Abilene-Paradox_The-Management-of-Agreement.htm_.pdf.

3.   Ignaz Semmelweis (1983) "The Etiology, Concept, and Prophylaxis of Childbed Fever," trans. K. Codell Carter Madison. Madison, WI: University of Wisconsin Press.

4.   Walter Scott. Cited on: BrainyQuote.com, *BrainyMedia* Inc, 2019. https://www.brainyquote.com/quotes/walter_scott_118003.

Chapter 9

1.   *American Psychological Association* (February 4, 2015) "Stress in America™: Paying With Our Health." https://www.apa.org/news/press/releases/stress/2014/stress-report.pdf.

2.   *The American Institute of Stress.* "What is Stress?" https://www.stress.org/daily-life.

3.   *The American Institute of Stress.* "What is Stress?" https://www.stress.org/daily-life.

4.   *American Academy of Child and Adolescent Psychiatry* (October 2017) "Suicide in Children and Teens." https://www.aacap.org/aacap/families_and_youth/facts_for_families/fff-guide/teen-suicide-010.aspx.

5.   Holly Hedegaard, Sally C. Curtin, and Margaret Warner (November 2018) "Suicide Mortality in the United States, 1999–2017," *Centers for Disease Control and Prevention.* https://www.cdc.gov/nchs/products/databriefs/db330.htm.

6.   Steve Connor (May 25, 2015) "The People Who Can't Feel Pain: Scientists Discover Cause of Rare Inherited Condition that Turns Off Pain Sensors," *Independent.*

https://www.independent.co.uk/life-style/health-and-families/health-news/the-people-who-cant-feel-pain-scientists-discover-cause-of-rare-inherited-condition-that-turns-off-10274604.html.

7. Tyler Joseph (2015) *Blurryface.* New York, NY: Fueled by Ramen LLC.

8. *American Psychological Association* (February 4, 2015) "Stress in America™: Paying With Our Health." https://www.apa.org/news/press/releases/stress/2014/stress-report.pdf.

9. Catey Hill (December 17, 2018) "This is the No. 1 Reason Americans are so Stressed Out," *Market Watch*.https://www.marketwatch.com/story/one-big-reason-americans-are-so-stressed-and-unhealthy-2018-10-11.

10. American Psychological Association (February 4, 2015)"Stress in America™: Paying With Our Health." https://www.apa.org/news/press/releases/stress/2014/stress-report.pdf.

Chapter 10

1. Bob Nelson (2012) *1501 Ways to Reward Employees.* New York, NY: Workman Publishing Company.

Chapter 12

1. Blaise Pascal (1847) *Letter XVI.* Cited in: *The Provincial Letters of Blaise Pascal, A New Translation with Historical Introduction And Notes By The Rev. Thomas M'Crie* .Ithaca, NY: Cornell University Library, p. 282.

2. E.L. Doctorow. Cited in: Charles Ruas (1985) *Conversations with American Writers.* NYC: Knopf, p. 211.

3. Stephen Covey (1989) *The 7 Habits of Highly Effective People.* New York, NY: Free Press, p. 235.

Chapter 15

1. Alexander Harris (March 11, 2019) "U.S. Self-storage Industry Statistics," *Sparefoot Storage Beat.* https://www.sparefoot.com/self-storage/news/1432-self-storage-industry-statistics.

2. Alexander Harris (March 11, 2019) "U.S. Self-storage Industry Statistics," *Sparefoot Storage Beat.* https://www.sparefoot.com/self-storage/news/1432-self-storage-industry-statistics.

Chapter 16

1. *Trading Economics* (February 2019) "France Tourism Revenues." https://trading-economics.com/france/tourism-revenues.

Chapter 18

1. Jimmy Carter (1995) *Keeping Faith: Memoirs of a President.* New York, NY: Bantam Books, pp. 408-409.

2. Lee G. Boleman and Terrance E. Deal (2017) *Reframing Organizations: Artistry, Choice, and Leadership.* Hoboken, NJ: Wiley.

3. Robert B. Cialdini (1993) *The Psychology of Persuasion, Six Principles of Persuasion.* New York, NY: William Morrow and Company.

Chapter 19

1. Quote Investigator (May 9, 2014). https://quoteinvestigator.com/2014/05/09/urgent.

Chapter 20

1. John Lennon (1980) *Beautiful Boy (Darling Boy).* Santa Monica, CA: Geffen Records.

2. Bonnie Ware (2012) *The Top Five Regrets of the Dying*. Carlsbad, CA: Hay House Inc.

3. Debbie Duarte. Cited in: Becky Bicks, *Improve Your Storytelling Presentation Skills and Get Your Ideas Adopted*. https://www.duarte.com/presentation-skills-resources/storytelling-presentation-skills/.

4. Viktor E. Frankl. Cited on: Goodreads.com. *https://www.goodreads.com/quotes/315385-those-who-have-a-why-to-live-can-bear-with*.

Acknowledgments

1. Friedrich Nietzsche (1878) *Human, All-Too-Human: Parts One and Two*. Mineola, NY: Dover, p. 105.